China's Assistance Program in Xinjiang

China's Assistance Program in Xinjiang

A Sociological Analysis

Yuhui Li

LEXINGTON BOOKS
Lanham • Boulder • New York • London

Published by Lexington Books
An imprint of The Rowman & Littlefield Publishing Group, Inc.
4501 Forbes Boulevard, Suite 200, Lanham, Maryland 20706
www.rowman.com

Unit A, Whitacre Mews, 26-34 Stannary Street, London SE11 4AB

British Library Cataloguing in Publication Information Available

Library of Congress Cataloging-in-Publication Data Available

LCCN 2018945970 | ISBN 9781498539395 (hardback : alk. paper) |
ISBN 9781498539401 (electronic)

∞™ The paper used in this publication meets the minimum requirements of American National Standard for Information Sciences—Permanence of Paper for Printed Library Materials, ANSI/NISO Z39.48-1992.

Printed in the United States of America

Contents

List of Tables

Acknowledgment

I wish to thank the College of Humanities and Social Sciences and the Provost Office at Rowan University for granting me adjusted teaching load to work on this research.

I spent much time doing research for this project in the East Asian Gest Library at Princeton University. I want to thank the staff there who were most helpful.

I have shared my research at meetings of the Central European Studies Society. I appreciate valuable feedback and input from colleagues at the meeting, particularly comments made by James Millward.

Additional thanks go to members of the editorial group of Lexington Books. I want to specifically thank Brian Hill, former acquisition editor of History and Asian Studies, for his initial suggestion of producing a manuscript based on my research on the current topic, as well as his patience and assistance when I was writing the book; Julia Torres for her diligence in overseeing the editing process of this book; and Joseph Gautham for his guidance and help in the production of this book.

Introduction

Significance of the Research

It is not an exaggeration to state that Xinjiang plays a decisive role in China's efforts to realize the "China Dream," which is an inspirational slogan that the Xi administration put forward to guide the future of China.[1] Xinjiang is the largest geographic territory in China. It shares borders with Russia, Mongolia, Kazakhstan, Kyrgyzstan, Tajikistan, Afghanistan, Pakistan, and India and connects China with central and southeastern Asia, which then extend to Africa and Europe. The strategically important position has a significant impact on not only China's diplomatic and foreign relations but also the ambitious One-Belt One-Road (OBOR) campaign,[2] which is the most ambitious project that China has launched to help achieve the China Dream. Furthermore, Xinjiang is rich in natural resources such as oil, coal, gas, and minerals, all of which are badly needed for China's continued economic development.

Despite these attractive features, there are serious problems and challenges in Xinjiang that hold the potential to become severe obstacles in China's efforts to achieve its expectations. A diverse region in terms of the population composition, Xinjiang is home to many ethnic populations that are culturally and socially as well as physiologically different from the dominant Han population in China. Numerous ethnic groups, particularly the Uyghur, have been attempting over decades to seek meaningful recognition of their ethnic identity and autonomy from China. These aspirations have led to periodic ethnic tension and conflict in Xinjiang, especially since the end of the 20th century.

Following the worst racial violence for decades in the region in 2009, which resulted in close to two hundred deaths and thousands injuried, the Chinese government made several moves to fundamentally address the racial tension in the region, with the most significant being the strengthening of an existing partnership assistance program between Xinjiang and the eastern and central parts of China. Starting from 2010, 19 provinces and municipalities in coastal and central regions of China, as well as departments directly under the central government, have been matched with various administrative divisions in Xinjiang as assistance partners. The provinces and municipalities were required to commit 0.3 to 0.6 percent of their respective annual revenues to the assistance program and deliver economic, technological, human capital, cultural, social welfare, and other resources to the recipient administrative units in Xinjiang for at least a decade starting from 2010.

The chain of events that led to the 2010 version of Xinjiang assistance program described above confirms numerous scholarly observations on developmental patterns and strategies of China in general and Xinjiang in particular. First, the heavy emphasis on financial and economic aspects in the program is yet another indicator that the Chinese government believes that economic development is an effective cure for all problems in the society, including racial tension. Second, the program reflects the Chinese government's teleological assumption of the country's continuous progress and improvement in its developmental trajectory. Under this assumption, Xinjiang is viewed as one of the regions with deficiencies and inadequacies and therefore it needs help to catch up with economically advanced areas. Finally, another noticeable pattern is that all decisions concerning the program are made by the central government and assistance delivering units.[3] Local communities and populations in Xinjiang, that is, target recipients of the assistance, have few, if any, opportunities to present their input concerning the program even though they are the ones who endure direct and serious consequences of the implementation of the program.

The expectation that economic progress brings social harmony and the assumption that interventional programs leads to the improvement of societal conditions are both controversial issues in social science research. An analysis of the Xinjiang assistance program and the dramatic social, economic, demographic, environmental, and other changes it has generated can help shed light on these postulations. It is important, however, to note that the analysis reflects perspectives of not only decision makers of the program, but also those who are on the receiving end of the assistance.

This current research engages in a comprehensive coverage of areas in Xinjiang that have been designated to receive the assistance. These areas include professional personnel, education, economic development, health care, and social welfare. The analysis addresses both macro-level changes such as the intensifying socioeconomic stratification in the region as well as micro-level dynamics and cultural patterns such as shifting social and racial relationships in an increasingly more urbanized and modernized Xinjiang. By examining dramatic changes that have been taking place as a result of the assistance program in the wide range of fields mentioned above, this research hopes to demonstrate the intensity, the broad scope as well as the magnitude of the impact that the assistance program has generated, and will continue to generate, in Xinjiang's social and natural landscapes.

In addition to the sociological analysis of affairs concerning Xinjiang assistance program at the contemporary time, this study also emphasizes historical and longitudinal changes of the various aspects of the program. Some of the historical origin in the assistance program could be traced to imperial China thousands of years ago and some reflect historical patterns of interactions between China and the former Soviet Union. The historical analysis of these phenomena and interactions offers important clues to the understanding of the official justification of the program as well as local responses, including resistance, to the program.

THEORETICAL FRAMEWORKS AND RESEARCH QUESTIONS

This research reviews numerous theoretical perspectives based on research in a wide range of social science disciplines conducted in many parts of the world. Some of the perspectives rationalize and defend interventional schemes such as the assistance program for their perceived capability of improving human conditions. Others critique such programs for engendering detrimental consequences to human and environmental conditions. Utopianist and modernization theories are examples of the former and have served as theoretical foundations for very many different types of interventional campaigns all over the world throughout the human history. They have been heavily used to guide the assistance program in Xinjiang as well.

However, scholars have repeatedly demonstrated the many negative consequences and frequent failure of interventional programs initiated by powerful agencies or organizations in many parts of the world since the earliest human history. One major reason for the failure of interventional schemes has to do with faulty ideological assumptions about human nature, human relationships, and the association between the natural environment and human societies. China's Great Leap Forward movement during the late 1950s and early 1960s and the Great Western Development Strategy (GWDS) that took place in China at the end of 2000s are both examples to illustrate this argument.

The main questions that are addressed in this book include the following: (1) What are theoretical foundations and conceptual frameworks that have served as the policy basis to guide the assistance program in Xinjiang and China? (2) What are the historical, political, and cultural characteristics in China and Xinjiang that have helped facilitate the institutionalization of the assistance program in Xinjiang? (3) How is the assistance program structured? What are the main components of the program and what is the rationale for focusing on these components? (4) How is the assistance program implemented? What mechanisms are employed to ensure the effectiveness of the implementation? What obstacles, if any, have been encountered in the assistance program? (5) What changes have taken place or are likely to take place in social, economic, demographic, political, environmental, and other areas that have resulted from the assistance program? (6) What are the theoretical implications of the assistance program in Xinjiang? Is it appropriate or feasible to apply the program model to other periphery settings or societies such as Tibet? (7) What lessons can we learn from Xinjiang assistance program about human and community development and its relationship with political, economic, and social structures?

DATA, METHODOLOGY, AND THEORETICAL FRAMEWORKS

It is important to point out that it has been difficult to conduct research in Xinjiang, for the Chinese government treats many issues within the realm of social science studies as sensitive topics and often may forbid them from being studied by academic researchers. Consequently, there is severe data inadequacy measuring sentiment concerning the assistance program by local populations in Xinjiang, especially minority populations. These feelings and opinions, however, can be gauged, very often indirectly, from published studies, policies and statements by governmental officials as well as official data sources described below.

In addition to a few personal interviews and observations conducted in Xinjiang over the past several years, the major data sources for this research are official publications in China, which include Xinjiang and China Yearbooks, Xinjiang and China Statistical Yearbooks, China Censuses, China Health Statistics, China Statistical Yearbooks for Regional Economy and Xinjiang Survey Data. Longitudinal data from these and other data sources are presented to support arguments made in relevant chapters. At one time, researchers were concerned about the quality of quantitative data generated in China. But these concerns seem to have become less of an issue as data generated in China are considered to be of better quality in recent years (Cai 2013).

In addition to statistical information, qualitative data based on personal interviews and observations in Xinjiang are also presented in various chapters. These interviews and observations took place over the last several years while visiting China. Some of the interviews were prearranged and interviewees had been informed of the purpose of the meetings. Some of the observations that are referred to in the discussion took place as casual conversations or interactions. But I believe they provided just as valid empirical information as formal interviews concerning issues addressed in the book.

The methodology used in this book is based on quantitative and qualitative data discussed above as well as analytical discussions of historical and contemporary issues that are relevant to the assistance program in Xinjiang. Whenever it is appropriate, a historical context is provided within which the analysis is conducted. Some of the historical episodes could be traced to thousands of years ago, and some are relatively more recent phenomena. The analysis of historical changes is important because it helps with the presentation of conceptual frameworks concerning the assistance program.

OVERVIEW OF CHAPTERS

The book consists of nine chapters. Following this introduction is the background chapter (chapter 1) on the history of Xinjiang and the Uyghur people, Xinjiang's geographic conditions, its demographics and economic characteristics, the importance of the Uyghur identity, the region's administrative structure, and other relevant information. This background discussion is essential to the analysis of the Xinjiang assistance program.

Chapter 2 discusses patterns of implementation of historical and contemporary assistance programs in PRC. The two regions of Tibet and Xinjiang have been the designated recipients of assistance from the central government and the rest of China since the founding of the PRC. The discussion in this chapter focuses on the rationale and chronological changes of the implementation of the assistance program in these two regions. This background information serves as way-paving material for the analysis of the most recent wave of assistance programs in Xinjiang since 2010.

Chapter 3 presents relevant theoretical perspectives pertinent to the assistance program in China. These include conceptual frameworks that have influenced developmental policies both before and after the reform in China, as well as theories that have impacted interventional policies in other social settings. Some of the perspectives reviewed in the chapter provide theoretical foundations for the implementation of the assistance program, while others challenge the rationale and justification of top-down interventional efforts such as the assistance program. The presentation of the opposing viewpoints helps to objectively frame the discussion on the assistance program in Xinjiang.

Chapter 4 focuses on cadre and personnel assistance in the Xinjiang assistance program. The analysis starts with patterns of personnel dispatch to Xinjiang by China's administration since the Qing dynasty (1644–1911). This is followed by the examination of specific strategies to lure cadre members and professionals to participate in the recent assistance program in Xinjiang. It will be demonstrated that there are tremendous similarities and overlapping in terms of both objectives and conditions for dispatching personnel to Xinjiang between dynastic periods in history and current assistance programs in Xinjiang.

Chapter 5 deals with economic assistance in the Xinjiang assistance program. Xinjiang has been the recipient of financial subsidies from the central government since before it officially became part of China in 1884. The continuous subsidies, however, have not brought Xinjiang's economy to the level of China's economically advanced regions. The amount of financial aid to Xinjiang since the start of the most recent wave of the assistance program in 2010 has been astronomical but it remains to be seen how the huge amount of financial support will affect the economy and other aspects of the region.

Chapter 6 addresses issues related to educational assistance to Xinjiang. The discussion focuses on changes of language policies in the region that have resulted in the rapid marginalization of minority languages within the educational system. By diminishing the minority language even more dramatically, which is often viewed by minority populations as an assault to their ethnic identity and culture, the assistance program is likely to further aggravate the situation of racial divide in the region, the very situation that the assistance program is intended to avoid.

Chapter 7 discusses the Xinjiang assistance program in health care and welfare programs such as residential housing construction. This type of assistance has generated probably the most direct and immediate results in improving the lives of Xinjiang residents. Thousands of medical professionals have been dispatched to Xinjiang, including rural areas, to deliver medical services and a tremendous amount of resources have been committed to the construction of new residential houses or renovation of existing ones, including those for farmers and nomadic populations. The sustainability of these welfare improvements, however, remains questionable.

Chapter 8 presents a case study of the assistance program in Xinjiang. Kashgar is a historical city and the largest urban center in southern Xinjiang. It carries tremendous significance both physically and symbolically for the Uyghur population, which is probably the reason the city has received more assistance compared with any other administrative units in Xinjiang. As a result, Kashgar has experienced dramatic changes in not only its physical landscape, but also social, economic, demographic, and cultural spheres. These changes carry such different connotations to the deliverers and recipients of the assistance that it is a challenge to assess them.

The concluding chapter presents an overall evaluation of the Xinjiang assistance program. A major goal of this chapter is to try to shed light on numerous controversial viewpoints that are embodied in the formulation and implantation of the assistance program. These viewpoints include, for example, the assumption that economic development and top-down interventional approaches are effective remedies to solve social problems such as racial tension and regional and racial inequalities. The outcomes of the implementation of programs based on these assumption, however, are heavily socially constructed. Additional research is needed to evaluate the unfolding assistance program in Xinjiang, particularly from the points of view of local populations, that is, recipients of the assistance.

NOTES

1. The idea of China Dream was first proposed by Mr. Xi Jinping as soon as he assumed power of the president of the Chinese Communist Party (CCP) in 2012. It is interpreted as the rejuvenation and revitalization of China in order to make it a rich and powerful nation (Ferdinand 2016; Callahan 2015).

2. OBOR is a campaign that was initiated by the Hu (Jintao) administration but was materialized by the Xi administration. It proposes to link China with central and southeast Asia, Africa, and Europe via economic and infrastructure corridors. For more detail on this topic, please see chapter 3.

3. Even though China has been practicing a market economy for four decades, politically it is still an authoritarian state. It is with this high concentration of state authority and political power that the central government is able to implement large-scale and costly campaigns such as the assistance program.

Chapter 1

Background of Xinjiang

Geography, History, Economy, Demographics, Uyghur Identity, and Administrative Structure

Xinjiang is not a typical province of China. It is huge in size, diverse in ethnic composition, and physically much closer to population centers across the border than to those in China proper. These are some of the reasons that made Xinjiang's integration with China difficult, even after Xinjiang officially became a province of China during the Qing Dynasty in the late 19th century. Different from its predecessors, the PRC government has been able to bring about major transformations that previous governments were not able to achieve. These transformations include large waves of Han migration to and settlement in the region, which subsequently resulted in a drastic change in the composition of ethnic populations (see Table 1.1), construction of infrastructures and modernization facilities such as highways that pass through the desert, establishment of an administrative structure in line with the nation's administrative system, and so on.

This chapter deals first with the geographic conditions of Xinjiang, which will be followed by a brief history of the interaction and relationship between Xinjiang and China proper. It will then discuss the administrative structure of Xinjiang and Xinjiang's demographic, social, and economic characteristics.

GEOGRAPHIC CONDITIONS OF XINJIANG

Xinjiang is the largest provincial-level unit in China in geographic territory. The area of Xinjiang's 1.6 million square kilometers constitutes one-sixth of China's total land territory. With a borderline of more than 5,300 kilometers, Xinjiang borders numerous countries with Mongolia and Russia to the north, Kazakhstan, Kyrgyzstan, and Tajikistan to the west, and Afghanistan, Pakistan and India to the southwest.

Xinjiang's geographic conditions are complex. The shape of Xinjiang looks like a slightly tilted rectangle, with the longer side facing inland China on the southeast edge and the other side facing the countries of Kazakhstan and Kyrgyzstan on the northwestern side. Further, Xinjiang is divided into two parts mostly by three ranges of mountains: the Altay Mountain range to the north, the Tianshan Mountain range in the middle, and the Kunlun, the Karakorum, and Pamir mountain ranges in the south. The area that lies between Altay and Tianshan Mountains is known as northern Xinjiang, and the area between Tianshan Mountain and the mountains in the south of the region is referred to as southern Xinjiang. The eastern part of Xinjiang that borders with Gansu Province, the only relatively easy pathway between Xinjiang and the rest of China, is referred to as eastern Xinjiang.

In addition to mountain ranges, the Jungar Basin makes up a significant part of northern Xinjiang. Large stretches of grasslands and many oasis towns and cities are distributed throughout the Jungar Basin in northern Xinjiang. Due to its relative proximity to China proper and comparatively more developed infrastructure and transportation facilities, particularly for the excavation of natural resources for industrial development such as oil and coal, northern Xinjiang is more industrialized and urbanized than the rest of Xinjiang. Urumqi, the capital city and the largest city of Xinjiang, and Karamey, one of China's major oil-producing centers, are both located in northern Xinjiang.

The Taklamakan Desert, which is the world's second largest desert, comprises much of southern Xinjiang. Most of the oasis towns in southern Xinjiang are located around the rim of the Desert, which was why transportation connecting the towns used to be costly and traveling in southern Xinjiang was very time consuming.[1] Some of the most important historical, cultural, and economic centers not only in Xinjiang but the whole of Central Asia, such as Kashgar and Hotan, are located in southern Xinjiang. Since the gradual shift of the world's major trade routes from land to sea starting from the 16th century, however, the former trade and cultural centers have lost their prominence and southern Xinjiang has become much less active economically compared with northern Xinjiang (see Table 1.2).

Eastern Xinjiang, which includes Hami and Turpan administrative offices, consists of a relatively small number of towns and populations in Xinjiang, as Table 1.2 illustrates. One of the most important aspects about eastern Xinjiang is that it is the pathway connecting Xinjiang and the rest of China.

BRIEF HISTORY OF XINJIANG

Geographically, Xinjiang constitutes a significant part of Central Asia. Even though Xinjiang did not officially become a part of China until the later part of the 19th century, the relationship between various territories of Central Asia and China could be traced to the Han Dynasty (206 BC–AD 220) of China (Di Cosmo 2009; Lattimore 1950; Millward 2007). As mentioned earlier, what was to be named "Xinjiang," which means new frontier land, was strategically located along the famous Silk Road. Many towns and cities along the Silk Road in Xinjiang were important economic, commercial, political, cultural, and military centers thousands of years ago, visited frequently by business people, tourists, scholars, governmental officials (many of who found themselves in the region because of their exiled status, as will be discussed in detail in chapter 4), religious missionaries, military personnel, and others, coming from all over the world. Many of these cities and towns, for instance, Hotan, Kashgar, Aksu, Kucha (Kuqa or Guizi), Turpan, and Ruoqiang (Qakilik), are still important economic and cultural centers in current Xinjiang.

Until the Qing Dynasty (1644–1912), China's control of and interaction with Xinjiang was sporadic and inconsistent. Historically, the area of Xinjiang had been the target of control by competing forces and empires such as nomadic tribes in northern Xinjiang and agrarian settlers in southern Xinjiang. In addition, external forces such as Tibetans, the Xiongnu,[2] Persians, Russians, and Mongolians all had a direct and indirect impact on the region.

Even though Islam currently is the dominant religion for a large proportion of the population in Xinjiang, Buddhism was once the most predominant religion in the region. The shift from Buddhism to Islam as the dominant religion took place slowly over several centuries (13th through the 17th centuries), which eventually led to the situation whereby nearly all Turkic populations in the region became Muslims. The Mongols, a major ethnic group in Xinjiang, are the exception. Xinjiang Mongols are descendants of the once powerful Mongol Jungar (also known as Dzungar or Zunghar) Empire, whose origin could be traced to the Mongol forces that conquered massive amounts of territories and expanded their influence throughout Asia and Europe during the 13th and 14th centuries. China's Yuan Dynasty (1271–1368), ruled by Mongols, was one of the few dynastic periods in China controlled by non-Chinese. However, the Jungar Empire in the Xinjiang region lingered as one of the last Mongol legacies after the Yuan Dynasty was replaced by the Han Chinese-ruled Ming Dynasty (1368–1644), a dynastic change that reflected the demise of the Mongol superpower globally. The Jungar Empire, however, ultimately collapsed during the mid-18th century as a result of years of intense and brutal campaigns by the army of China's Qing Dynasty, the last imperial dynasty of China.

After defeating the Jungar Mongols, the Qing government of China, represented by General Zuo Zongtang, made two moves that have had a long-lasting impact on not only Xinjiang, but also China and nearby regions.

First, the area in Central Asia adjacent to China, called *Xiyu* (meaning Western Territory) by China since ancient times, was renamed Xinjiang (meaning New Territory). Second, in 1884, Xinjiang was officially classified as one of China's provinces by the Qing government. The official designation of Xinjiang as part of China was not without resistance from local ethnic groups, especially Muslim Turkic populations. Besides, there was heavy interference from the Russian across the border as part of the attempt to sabotage China's control of Xinjiang (Millward 2007).

From the end of the Qing Dynasty until the founding of the PRC, Xinjiang mostly was left alone while China was deeply involved in civil wars and chaotic battles. However, one significant episode that took place during this period had had a long-lasting impact on the affairs of Xinjiang. During the early 20th century, a large number of various Turkic ethnic populations was collectively designated as "Uyghur." Previously, these Turkic populations had been considered culturally distinctive ethnic groups in the region (Thum 2014).[3]

The term "Uyghur," meaning "civilization" (Brophy 2016) seemed to be initially associated with a state, rather than an ethnic group. The Uyghur Empire (745–840) was one of the many forces that competed for power and territory in the Central Asian region. After the demise of the empire, its various diaspora were referred to as Uyghur (Millward and Perdue 2004; Rudelson and Jankowiak 2004). However, "Uyghur" was not a popular or official designation for these people until the 1930s. Under the influence of Soviet ethnic policies and ethnographic practices (Hsieh 1986; Millward and Tursun 2004), the then governor of Xinjiang, Mr. Sheng Shicai, who was known for being heavily manipulated by the Soviets, decided to adopt the name "Uyghur" to refer to a large number of Muslim ethnic groups in Xinjiang.[4] Even though this governmental action generated strong objections from leaders of Turkic populations in Xinjiang, who preferred the term "Turkic" to describe their ethnic identity, "Uyghur" has since become the increasingly accepted designation when referring to Turkic populations, both officially as well as by the general population, in Xinjiang.[5]

Shortly after the Communist Party gained control of China in 1949, Xinjiang was "liberated" without much bloodshed. A series of campaigns were then launched in China to design ethnic policies and establish administrative structures in areas populated by ethnic minorities. As part of national ethnic policies, five autonomous regions for ethnic minorities were established in China: Tibetan (Xizang) Autonomous Region, Mongolian Autonomous Region, Ningxia Hui Autonomous Region, Guangxi Zhuang Autonomous Region, and Xinjiang Uyghur Autonomous Region.

That Xinjiang was made a Uyghur autonomous region, rather than an autonomous region of any other ethnic population who resided in the region, indicated that the new regime of China endorsed Governor Sheng Shicai's classification of "Uyghur" to embrace a large number of diverse Turkic populations. It also suggested that the PRC's ethnic policies were very much in line with an instrumentalist perspective, as indicated in the study of race and ethnicity (Harrell 1990).[6] Most importantly, and perhaps unexpectedly, these policies have played the role of strengthening the Uyghur population's ethnic identity and the surge of Uyghur nationalism that Xinjiang has been experiencing since the end of the last century (Bovingdon 2002; Smith 2000).

UYGHUR IDENTITY

With a total population of about ten million people, the Uyghur is one of the major Muslim populations in China. Also, there are numerous sizeable Uyghur communities in Central Asian countries across from the border from Xinjiang (Roberts 2004). The Uyghurs in and outside of China have developed their own ethnic identity and cultural patterns that reflect their historical origins which could be traced to even prior to the spread of Islamic religion to the region (Thum 2014). And it is through a unique approach that the Uyghur people create and share their history, which helps enhance their ethnic identity.

In many Islamic communities, manuscripts written by respected Islamic scholars are deemed as important legacies and have been preserved, reproduced, and taught to generations of students and disciples (Bradley 2015). The Uyghur is no exception to this tradition. Various types of books, scripts, and other literary artifacts concerning Uyghur (Altishahr) history have been produced and widely circulated in the Uyghur culture through not only formally educational channels, but, more importantly, pragmatic methods such as pilgrimage to shrines and even recitations at the bazaar (Thum 2014). All these methods significantly enhanced the effectiveness of delivery as well as accessibility of scripts regarding Uyghur history and morality, Uyghur's attitude toward the nature, and so on. As Thum comments, these practices have resulted in the "construction of a particular kind of identity system in Altishahr, an imagined community" (Thum 2014, 134).

In addition to what Thum refers to as "sacred routes of Uyghur history" (Thum 2014), many global events since the beginning of the 20th century have also influenced the Uyghur culture and identity. The collapse of the Ottoman Empire resulted in the weakening of the influence of the Turkic culture and civilization, which was further aggravated by the success of the Russian revolution. The demise of the Qing Dynasty and subsequent decades of civil war in China brought a tremendous amount of turmoil to the country, including Xinjiang. The Uyghur suffered extreme mistreatment by various warlords and governmental officials who ruled Xinjiang during the early part of the 20th century (Smith 2000).

As will be discussed in the following chapters, ethnic policies, and their changes, as well as political, economic, and social structures of the PRC have influenced the Uyghur culture and identity in a complicated fashion. One of the most intriguing research results concerning Uyghur identity in the PRC is that there is a correlation between socioeconomic status and occupational categories of the Uyghur people on the one hand and how they express their ethnic identities on the other hand. Uyghur peasants tend to consider themselves Muslims before any other cultural categories. Intellectuals view their association with Turkic culture as the most significant part of their identity whereas Uyghur merchants tend to accept being Chinese as the most salient aspect of their identity (Rudelson 1998). These research results demonstrate the heterogeneity of the Uyghur population in terms of their culture and identities.

The declaration of independence by former Soviet territories across the border from Xinjiang at the end of the 20th century and the global campaign of war against Islamic terrorism at the beginning of the 21st century have been even more influential factors shaping Uyghur culture and identity. These events served as impetus for the surge of Uyghur nationalism and ethnic identity. China's subsequent efforts to quell these movements, particularly after the 2009 riots, have further complicated the situation concerning the identity of Uyghur people. While the state of affairs resulting from China's policies in Xinjiang is still unfolding, one thing that is certain is that Uyghurs in and outside of China will continue creating and sharing their own history. After all, the Uyghur, just like many other ethnic groups in Xinjiang and the Central Asian region, have a long tradition of engaging in cross-border trade, intellectual communication, religious activities, and educational reforms, all of which have helped enhance their community solidarity and their "oasis identity" (Brophy 2016; Rudelson and Jankowiak 2004).

ADMINISTRATIVE STRUCTURE AND THE DEMOGRAPHIC CHANGES IN XINJIANG

As a designated Uyghur autonomous region, Xinjiang has experienced unique structural, demographic, and administrative changes. First, Xinjiang's population is one of the smallest among all provincial-level units in China, but it has increased rapidly in the last six or so decades. With a more than four-fold growth from 4.7 million during the early 1950s to the current 23 million, as is illustrated in Table 1.1, the overall population in Xinjiang has increased more than twice as fast as the population in China as a whole. In addition, there has been a high level of volatility in the change of Xinjiang's population. The increase of the population was much more dramatic prior to the

Table 1.1 Demographic Characteristics of Xinjiang, 1953–2010

	1953		*1964*		*1982*		*1990*		*2000*		*2010*	
	Xinj.	*China*	*Xinj.*	*China*	*Xinj.*	*China*	*Xinj.*	*China*	*Xinj.*	*China*	*Xinj.*	*China*
Tot pop. (millions)	4.7*	594.3	7.2	694.5	13.0	1008	15.1	1133	18.4	1265	22.09	1314
% change	–	–	4.8	1.5	4.4	2.5	1.8	1.5	2.2	1.6	1.26	0.57
Ethn (%)												
Han	6.9*	93.9	31.9	94.2	40.3	93.3	37.5	91.9	40.5	91.6	38.9.	91
Uyghur	75.4*	–	54.9*	–	45.4*	–	47.5	–	45.7	–	46.4	–

Source: *Almanac of China's Population* 2011.
*Zhou, 1990.

third census of 1982 compared with more recent decades. The population surge during the early years of the PRC was mostly a result of influxes of Han migration into the region from other parts of China (Ren and Yuan 2003; Toops 2004).

Second, the constant in-migration of Han population into Xinjiang has drastically changed the ethnic make-up of Xinjiang's population, as is shown in Table 1.1. The two largest ethnic groups in Xinjiang at the current time are the Uyghur and the Han, which comprise around 46 percent and 38 percent of Xinjiang's population, respectively. Yet as recently as 1953, at least three-quarters of Xinjiang's population was Uyghur and the Han made up only 7 percent of the population in Xinjiang. The second largest ethnic group in Xinjiang in 1953 was Kazaks which comprised 10 percent of Xinjiang's population and the Han was the third largest ethnic group at that time (Toops 2004).[7] It is predicted by many that the Han would surpass the Uyghur and become the largest ethnic group in Xinjiang in the near future (Becquelin 2004).

Third, based on the Stalinist/Soviet model of ethnic policies, all ethnic groups in China were to be recognized, identified and represented by the state according to the criteria of a geographic boundary, the same language, the common economy, and shared psychological characteristics (Harrell 1990, 517). Within the Xinjiang Uyghur Autonomous Region, aside from the Uyghur and Han, there were a large number of ethnic minority groups including the Kazak, the Mongol, the Hui, the Xibo, the Tajik, the Uzbek, the Kyrgyz, the Tatar, the Russian, and others. After much debate and negotiation, autonomous prefectures and counties were designated for various ethnic populations throughout the Uyghur autonomous region. Table 1.2 shows, for instance, that there are two Mongol autonomous prefectures (Bortala and Bayangol), one Hui autonomous prefecture (Changji), and one Kyrgiz autonomous prefecture (Kizilsu) within Xinjiang.[8]

XINJIANG PRODUCTION AND CONSTRUCTION CORPS (XPCC)

Xinjiang Production and Construction Corps, also known as Bingtuan, is a semi-military organization that was established in Xinjiang during the early 1950s. Initially, this organization consisted of mostly former military personnel who were discharged from military duties at the end of the civil war when Xinjiang was "liberated" during the early 1950s. These military personnel have since been joined by waves of Han migrants, which is the major reason that Bingtuan is often viewed by researchers as the mechanism that China uses to colonize Xinjiang (Becquelin 2000; Seymour 2000).

Table 1.2 Administrative Structure^ and Demographic and Socioeconomic Characteristics of Xinjiang's Prefecture-Level Units (2014)

Region	*Prefectural-Level Unit*	*# County-Level Units & Districts*	*GDP/capita (Yuan)*	*Pop.⁺ (1,000)*	*% Urban*	*Doctors/10,000*
Total	15	94	40,648	23,225.6	46.07	23.84
Northern Xinjiang	Urumqi*	7	70,428	2,669.1	97.12	50.16
	Karamay*	4	153,084	295.8	99.99	40.70
	Shihezi (XPCG)*	1	81,370	637.2	99.99	40.21
	(Yili Kazak Aut. Pre)	(24)	32,825	(4736.4)	61.27	22.95
	Yili	10	26,453	3,009.1	56.29	21.75
	Tacheng Ad. Office.^	7	44,851	1051.5	78.33	23.25
	Altay Ad. Office.^	7	35,932	675.8	56.91	27.80
	Changji Hui Auton. Prefecture	8	66,005	1,412.6	85.43	29.87
	Bortala Mongol Auton. Prefecture	3	52,448	493.9	80.91	30.15
Subtotal		47		1,0245		
Southern Xinjiang	Bayangol Mongol Auton. Prefecture	9	79,055	1,398.7	78.83	27.34
	Aksu Ad. Office.^	9	29,293	2,530.5	63.71	13.64
	Kizilsu Kyrgiz Autono. Prefecture	4	15,222	596.4	58.77	20.09
	Kashgar Ad. Office.^	11	16,024	4,488.2	37.55	12.78
	Hotan Ad. Office.^	8	8,993	2,258.2	34.99	12.14
Subtotal		41		11,272		
Eastern Xinjiang	Hami Ad. Office.^	3	65,646	616.9	88.68	31.74
	Turpan Ad. Office.^	3	40,457	653.1	72.21	22.37
Subtotal		6		1,270		

Note: The last column of the table shows number of medical personnel per every 10,000 people.
Source: Statistical Yearbook of Xinjiang.
*Prefecture-Level Cities.
^Administrative Offices are terms used to refer to prefecture-level administrative units in ethnic minority areas such as Xinjiang in China.
⁺Populations of listed prefecture-level administrative units do not add up to the total population listed in the table due to the omission of data for several relatively new XPCC cities that have been added to the data in the statistics yearbook. (See discussion below about XPCC).

In terms of power distribution, the XPCC is parallel to Xinjiang Uyghur Autonomous Region within China's hierarchy of administrative structure. In other words, just like all other provincial-level administrative units, the XPCC directly reports to the central government of China. The XPCC is composed of 14 divisions distributed throughout Xinjiang with a total population of 2.5 million, which makes up about 13 percent of Xinjiang's population.

Prior to 2010, the XPCC did not receive much attention in the assistance program. Things have changed since then. Nearly the whole XPCC organization was included into the list of administrative units to receive assistance when the 2010 assistance program was implemented. The administrative units that delivered the assistance are responsible for both the civilian and XPCC divisions in the respective districts or regions that they are assigned.

SOCIOECONOMIC STATUS AND DEMOGRAPHIC CHARACTERISTICS OF NORTHERN XINJIANG

Xinjiang's population of 23 million people is distributed in the area of 1.6 million square kilometers, resulting in the average population density in Xinjiang being only 13 persons per square kilometer (the national average of population density in China is 110 persons per square kilometer). Seven of the fifteen prefecture-level administrative units are in northern Xinjiang, five in southern Xinjiang and two in eastern Xinjiang. Table 1.2 lists the fifteen prefecture-level units in the three subregions of Xinjiang, as well as their geographic distributions, socioeconomic development levels and demographic characteristics.

According to Table 1.2, nearly half (44 percent) of Xinjiang's population resides in northern Xinjiang. All three prefecture-level cities in Xinjiang are located in northern Xinjiang. They are (1) Urumqi, the region's capital, (2) Karamay, an oil-producing center, and (3) the city of Shihezi, which is affiliated with XPCC. In addition, the following prefecture-level administrative units are also located in northern Xinjiang: (1) Yili Kazak Autonomous Prefecture (IKAP), (2) Changji Hui Autonomous Prefecture, and (3) Bortala Mongol Autonomous Prefecture. The IKAP, with a total population of more than 4 million people, is further divided into three districts: Yili District, Tacheng (Tarbagatai) District, and Altay Administrative Offices. Each of the three districts or offices further consists of various numbers of counties or county-level cities. Changji Hui Autonomous Prefecture has eight counties or county-level cities with a total population of 1.5 million. Bortala Mongol Autonomous Prefecture is the smallest prefecture-level unit that is not a city in Xinjiang in terms of population size. Its population is slightly less than half a million and distributed between two counties and one county-level city.

The economic development level of northern Xinjiang, measured in terms of GDP per capita, is much more advanced compared with the rest of Xinjiang, as is shown in Table 1.2. The three prefecture-level cities of Urumqi, Karamay, and Shihezi have a much higher GDP per capita compared with most other districts in Xinjiang in 2014. For example, Karamay's GDP of 153,084 yuan per capita is nearly four times higher compared with the average GDP per capita of 40,648 yuan in Xinjiang in general. The GDP per capita of Urumqi (70,428 yuan), the capital city, is nearly twice as high as the average GDP per capita of Xinjiang.

In addition, Table 1.2 also shows that northern Xinjiang is much more urbanized compared with southern Xinjiang. Indeed, all prefecture-level units in northern Xinjiang have a higher urbanization level compared with the average urbanization level in Xinjiang. For example, the proportion of urban population in Yili is lowest in northern Xinjiang. But even Yili's urbanization level of 56 percent (in both Yili District and Altay Administrative Office) is much higher compared with Xinjiang in general, which is 46.07 percent.

Finally, the last column of Table 1.2 lists the ratio of the number of doctors to a fixed number of residents. On average, there are 23.84 doctors for every 10,000 residents in Xinjiang. With the exception of two units (21.75 for Yili and 23.25 for Tacheng, both are part of Yili Kazak Autonomous Prefecture), all other prefectures and administrative offices in northern Xinjiang have more doctors out of 10,000 population compared with the average figure for Xinjiang. Table 1.2 also shows that cities tend to have more doctors in proportion to the population compared with prefectures and other types of administrative units. The city of Urumqi has more doctors in proportion to the population (50.16) compared with any other units, followed by Karamay and Shihezi with about 40 doctors in both cities.

SOCIOECONOMIC STATUS AND DEMOGRAPHIC CHARACTERISTICS OF SOUTHERN XINJIANG

Table 1.2 shows that there are slightly more people in southern Xinjiang (48 percent of the total population in the region) compared with northern Xinjiang. Kashgar Administrative Office, one of the five prefecture-level administrative units in southern Xinjiang with a population of 4.4 million people, is the largest prefecture-level unit in Xinjiang in terms of population size. Aksu Administrative Offices, with a population of 2.5 million people, is also one of the largest prefecture-level administrative units, followed by Hotan Administrative Offices, the southern-most district in Xinjiang with a population of 2.2 million. Finally, Bayangol and Kizilsu autonomous prefectures for Mongol and Kirgiz ethnic nationalities, respectively, are the smallest demographic units in the region with 1.3 million and 596 thousand people respectively.

With the only exception of Bayangol Mongol Autonomous Prefecture, the economic development level in southern Xinjiang is significantly lower compared with the rest of Xinjiang. When ranked according to GDP per capita, four out of the five prefectures or administrative offices in southern Xinjiang (Kashgar, Kizilsu, Hotan, and Aksu) are at or near the bottom of all administrative units. The GDP per capita of Hotan (8,993 yuan), the poorest region in Xinjiang, is less than a quarter of the average figure for Xinjiang overall, which is 40,648 yuan in 2014. The GDP per capita in Kizilsu (15,222 yuan), Kashgar (16,024 yuan), and Aksu (29,293 yuan) is also significantly lower compared to the regional average GDP value, according to Table 1.2.

That southern Xinjiang suffers from a low level of economic development is also addressed by other studies. Chao-yo Cheng, for example, lists the distribution of poverty-stricken counties in the region based on the state-stipulated criteria. Out of the total of 27 poverty-stricken counties in Xinjiang in 2010, 21, or 77 percent, are located in southern Xinjiang with 8 in Kashgar, 7 in Hotan, 4 in Kizilsu, and 2 in Aksu (Cheng 2011).

Southern Xinjiang's economically underdeveloped nature is further compounded by the relative inadequacy and lower status measured in terms of social and welfare indicators such as urbanization level, medical services, and personnel. According to Table 1.2, only about one-third of residents in Hotan (34.99 percent) and Kashgar (37.55 percent) are classified as urban, which is significantly lower compared with the regional average of 46.07 percent. Actually, these two prefectures are the only administrative units at this level in Xinjiang that have less than half of their populations being classified as urban.

Finally, health care services in southern Xinjiang are staffed with much fewer numbers of doctors in proportion to the population compared with the rest of Xinjiang. While the average number of doctors every 10,000 people in Xinjiang as a whole is 23.84, the number of doctors every 10,000 population for Hotan, Kashgar, Aksu and Kizilsu is 12.14, 12.78, 13.64, and 20.09, respectively, as is shown in the last column of Table 1.2. In other words, four out of five administrative units in southern Xinjiang have fewer doctors per 10,000 people compared with the regional average figure.

CORRELATION BETWEEN SOCIOECONOMIC STRATIFICATION AND RACIAL COMPOSITION IN XINJIANG

The regional variations between northern and southern Xinjiang in terms of their socioeconomic status discussed above are closely related to the distribution of ethnic populations, as is illustrated in Table 1.3. Listing the distribution of major ethnic groups in Xinjiang as well as the 15 prefecture-level

Table 1.3 Percentage of Major Ethnic Populations in Prefecture-Level Administrative Units in Xinjiang (2014)

		%					
Region	*Prefectural-Level Unit*	*Uyghur*	*Han*	*Kazak*	*Hui*	*Kyrgiz*	*Mongol*
Regional		45.7	39.7	7	4	.8	.8
Northern Xinjiang	Urumqi	13.7	72.1	2.5	9.9		0.4
	Karamay	15.5	74.7	4.1	2.5		0.9
	Shihezi (XPCG)	1.5	92.4	0.7	4.1		0.1
	(Yili Kazak Aut. Pre)	17.3	41.5	26.5	9.2	0.5	1.6
	Yili	25.6	36.5	21.1	10.8	0.7	1.2
	Tacheng Ad. Office.	4.7	56.4	25.6	8.1	0.2	3.3
	Altay Ad. Office	1.4	40.5	52.3	3.7		0.9
	Changji Hui Aut Prefect.	4.8	72.3	10.4	10.4		0.5
	Bortala Mon Prefect.	13.9	64.6	10.2	4.3		5.8
Southern Xinjiang	Bayangol Mon Prefect.	34.5	55.6	0.1	5.2		3.8
	Aksu Ad. Office	79.7	18.9	0	0.6	0.5	
	Kizilsu Kyrgiz Aut Prefec.	65	7.3	0	0.1	26.5	
	Kashgar Ad. Office	91.9	6.6	0	0.1	0.1	
	Hetian Ad. Office	96.3	3.5	0	0.1		
Eastern Xinjiang	Hami Ad. Office	17.7	68.7	9.5	3.0		0.5
	Turpan Ad. Office	72.6	21.2	0.1	5.9		

Source: Statistical Yearbook of Xinjiang, 2015.

administrative units, Table 1.3 shows that there is a correlation between regional variation and the distribution of the Han and minority ethnic groups. While the Uyghur population tends to concentrate in southern Xinjiang, with 96, 92, and 80 percent of residents in Hotan, Kashgar, and Aksu respectively being Uyghur, for example, the three cities of Shihezi, Karamay, and Urumqi in northern Xinjiang are predominantly inhabited by the Han population that makes up 92, 74, and 72 percent of their residents, respectively. Kizilsu Kyrgiz Autonomous Prefecture, one of the southern prefectures with the lowest socioeconomic development level in Xinjiang, is also predominantly inhabited by ethnic minority populations, since, according to the table, the Uyghur and the Kyrgiz, in combination, make up close to 92 percent of its population.

Researchers have studied the correlation between racial composition and the socioeconomic status of residents in communities in Xinjiang. Chaudhuri's research (2005) shows, for example, that there is a pattern of educational achievement and occupational characteristics by various ethnic groups in Xinjiang. The Han, the Mongol, and the Hui tend to have a more advanced educational level and be employed in governmental office and social service types of jobs. The Uyghur, the Kazak, and the Kyrgiz, on the other hand, tend to have a lower educational level and are more likely to be employed in agricultural sectors.

EASTERN XINJIANG

The administrative offices of Hami and Turpan in eastern Xinjiang, with populations of slightly more than half a million each, often are considered part of northern Xinjiang since they are located at a similar latitude with areas of northern Xinjiang. While Turpan's GDP per capita of 40,457 yuan is similar to the regional average value, Hami's economy is much stronger with a per capital GDP of 65,646 yuan. There is a consistent pattern of the correlation between racial composition and economic development level discussed above. Turpan, with a low GDP per capita, is a predominantly Uyghur region (72.6 percent). Hami has a much stronger economy and is a predominantly Han region with close to 69 percent of its population being Han.

SUMMARY

Xinjiang is not a typical province in China. Remote and vast, it is inhabited by diverse ethnic populations. Not surprisingly, maintaining racial relations has been a challenge for rulers of the region and China throughout history.

The issue has become even more acute due to the escalating racial divide in terms of socioeconomic status with ethnic minorities suffering from a significantly lower socioeconomic status compared with the Han. In addition, the strong desire for self-rule and autonomy expressed by minority populations in recent years has further complicated the situation.

The implementation of the large-scale assistance program in Xinjiang since 2010 is partly to address the racial tension in the region. More importantly, it was to enhance China's state-building capabilities. In order to fully understand the rationale of the implementation of the program, an overview of the assistance program is necessary, which is the topic of the next chapter.

NOTES

1. Two highways were constructed through the Taklimakan desert during the 1990s and 2000s. One links the cities of Aksu and Hotan and the other links the towns of Qiemo and Luntai. These highways are among the longest in the world across shifting-sand desert and they have made travel in southern Xinjiang much easier and less costly.

2. Xiongnu was a nomadic population in ancient China that constantly raided northern China (Di Cosmo 1994, 1106–1109). The Chinese regarded the Xiongnu as one of the most "barbarous" ethnic groups (Fu 2014, 175–180). The Great Wall of China was constructed more than two thousand years ago for national defense purposes against aggressions from the north (Fu 2014, 104–105).

3. According to Perdue, the Uyghur in Yili area, referred to as "Taranchi," were recruited by the Qing government from southern Xinjiang to populate the Jungar region after the Mongols there were practically exterminated. Taranchi's rich experience in agricultural cultivation helped with land reclamation in the Jungar region. Since there were differences in political, economic social, demographic and cultural features between northern and southern Xinjiang, the Taranchi have developed their own cultural patterns that are different from the Uyghur in southern Xinjiang (Perdue 2005, 344–345, 352–357).

4. See Hsieh for the formation and development of China's ethnic nationality policies. Hsieh outlines the four criteria that China borrowed from the Soviets to define a nationality or ethnic group: (1) common language, (2) similar economic production mode and patterns, (3) unique cultural characteristics, and (4) psychological identity. These criteria probably served as the foundation for Sheng's decision.

5. This popularly held view about Russian's predominant role in the designation of Uyghur ethnic group in Xinjiang has been challenged by researchers, however. Roberts, for example, argues that it was Uyghur intellectuals and the anti-colonial and nationalist sentiment that played the most instrumental role in establishing the Uyghur nation (Roberts 2009).

6. Social scientists have been debating between the primordialist and instrumentalist perspectives in the study of race/ethnicity. The former emphasizes roles played by

individual ethnic groups and members, viewing them as actors and participants who are actively involved in their own affairs, their designation, and their status in the society. In contrast, the latter perspective regards issues concerning ethnicity as part of economic, political, and social structures. In other words, the former is a bottom-up approach, with full regard to members and groups of ethnic variations, while the latter is a top-down approach, with primary consideration devoted to arrangement and changes of social and economic establishment that are usually dictated by the state (Harrell 1990).

7. The Kazak is now the third largest ethnic group in Xinjiang that composes 7 percent of the region's population.

8. In addition, there are six autonomous counties in various prefectures and administrative districts in Xinjiang: Barkol Kazak Autonomous County in Hami District, Mori Kazak Autonomous County in Changji Hui Autonomous Prefecture, Qapqal Xibe Autonomous County and Hoboksar Mongol Autonomous County in Yili Kazak Autonomous Prefecture, Yanji Hui Autonomous County in Bayangol Mongol Autonomous Prefecture, and Taxkorgan Tajik Autonomous County in Kashgar District.

Chapter 2

Partnership Assistance Programs in China and Xinjiang

The idea of partnership assistance was initially brought forward in China as early as the 1950s and 1960s. The primary reason for the loosely structured efforts of partnership assistance during the early years of the PRC was to help improve the "underdeveloped" conditions of remote areas predominantly inhabited by ethnic minorities, such as Tibet and Xinjiang, in western China. Numerous Han provinces and municipalities in the coastal and central regions were called upon to participate in the assistance programs (News SINA 2010.05.04).

The beginning of the economic reform at the end of the 1970s saw the process of intensified institutionalization of assistance programs. A National Defense Work Conference (全国边防工作会议) was held in Beijing in April 1979 with the major goal of searching for the most effective strategy to speed up the construction of frontier areas inhabited mostly by ethnic minorities. Mr. Ulanhu, the then president of the Department of the United Front Work (统战部) in China, delivered a keynote speech titled "The People of the Whole Country Unite and Strive for the Prosperity and Construction of Borderline Areas and for the Consolidation of Border Defense." Based on the speech, a document titled "The Central Government Policy Number 52" was produced at the meeting. It stipulated the need for provinces and municipalities in the eastern part of China to assist the development of frontier and ethnic minority areas. The document also published the official formation of the following pairs of partnership involved in assistance programs (see Table 2.1): Beijing municipality assisting Inner Mongolia Autonomous Region, Hebei Province assisting Guizhou Province, Jiangsu Province assisting both Guangxi Zhuang and Xinjiang Uyghur Autonomous Regions, Shandong Province assisting Qinghai Province, Shanghai Municipality assisting both

Yunnan Province and Ningxia Hui Autonomous Region, and the whole country assisting Tibet Autonomous Region (Zhao, M. 2011).

As can be seen from the arrangement of paired partners listed in Table 2.1, all areas at the receiving end of the assistance programs were predominantly inhabited by ethnic minorities whereas all provinces and municipalities delivering the assistance were located in the coastal region (with the exception of assistance to Tibet). In other words, assistance programs are measures to address regional as well as racial and ethnic inequalities in China. Not surprisingly, therefore, the continued formalization and institutionalization of assistance programs took place within the realm of ethnic minority policies.

In May of 1984, at the second session of the sixth National People's Congress, a legal document was passed with the title "the Laws of Autonomous Regions of Ethnic Minorities of PRC" (*minzu quyu zizhifa*) (NPC 2001). It was the first comprehensive legal document concerning autonomous areas of ethnic minorities in China. The last chapter of this document, Chapter 6, addresses responsibilities of higher authorities in regard to leadership roles they were expected to play in facilitating the development of minority areas. One of the items, Item Number 61, states, "Higher authorities should organize and encourage economic and technological collaborations between developed areas and ethnic autonomous areas and the former should help increase the levels of management and productivity of the latter" (NPC 2001). With such stipulations, this document made it a legal obligation for Han-dominant areas to deliver assistance to ethnic minority areas based on the government's assessment and plans. In other words, the document gave governmental agencies at various levels of the authority to organize and implement programs and campaigns for the purposes of revenue sharing and assistance delivery between Han and minority areas whenever and wherever the government sees the need to do so (Zhao, M. 2011).

In addition to official institutionalization and formal legalization, assistance programs and related policies also received affirmative recognition based on remarks from leaders in China, which helped further enhance its legitimacy. In September 1988, when addressing the concern regarding

Table 2.1 Matching Partners of the Assistance Program in China, 1979

Assistance-Delivery Units	*Assistance Receiving Units*
Beijing	Inner Mongolia Autonomous Region
Hebei	Guizhou Province
Jiangsu	Guangxi Zhuang and Xinjiang Uyghur Autonomous Regions
Shandong	Qinghai Province
Shanghai	Yunnan Province and Ningxia Hui Autonomous Region
The Whole Country	Tibetan Autonomous Region

escalating regional inequalities in China as a result of the reform, Mr. Deng Xiaoping, the paramount leader of China at the time, was quoted as having conceptualized the ideas of "two general situations" (*liangge daju*) in China's developmental policies. The first situation referred to the endorsement of the coastal region experiencing rapid economic growth with favorable conditions and preferential policies provided by the central government. Mr. Deng was quoted to have argued that once the economy of the coastal region becomes developed and advanced, it would then have the obligation and responsibility to help and assist less developed regions and areas, which would constitute the second general situation.

In early 1992, during a visit to southern China that had spearheaded the economic reform, Deng reiterated the need to continuously implement policies based on his theories of two general situations. Deng had to repeatedly emphasize these points because he was aware that his theory of tiered economic development model was highly controversial (Vogel 2011, 670–681; Zhao, S. 1993). The escalating inequality between the coastal and inland areas resulting from economic policies based on Deng's comments generated resentment and resistance from both provincial and local officials as well as the general public, especially in non-coastal regions (Creed and Liu 2014). Deng ultimately prevailed in having his economic policies implemented. As a consequence, the coastal region of China experienced a huge economic boom, which led to further economic and social disparities between the coast and the inland areas of China.

That ethnic minority areas lagged behind the rest of China in terms of economic development was believed to be one of the major contributing factors for the widespread anger of ethnic minority populations in China during the 1990s (Dreyer 2003; Wong 2010). This perception played a major role in the promotion of the argument by the government that the most effective recipe to resolve the problem of racial tension was to stimulate the economic development in the western region. As a result, in addition to launching the Great Western Development Strategy (GWDS) at the end of the 1990s,[1] existing partnership assistance programs were intensified in Tibet and Xinjiang in order to achieve the goal of stimulating the local economy and reducing regional economic disparities in the country.

ASSISTANCE PROGRAM IN TIBET

As was discussed earlier, when the assistance program in China became formalized and institutionalized during the reform, Tibet was the only designated region to receive assistance from the whole country, while all other areas would be assisted only one province or municipality. There were several reasons for Tibet to receive the special attention in this version of the assistance program. In addition to its drastically different economic, geographic, social, and demographic characteristics from the rest of China, the political instability of Tibet since the early years of the PRC was probably a dominant factor.[2]

One of the earliest major events that happened in Tibet after it was taken over by the CCP was the construction of two major highways connecting Tibet and adjacent provinces of Qinghai to the northeast of Tibet and Sichuan to the east of Tibet. It was through these highways that most of the assistance materials and personnel were transported to Tibet. The assistance provided by the central government and cities and provinces in eastern China focused primarily on infrastructure, such as oil pipelines, airports, bridges and factories, and welfare programs (Fischer 2009). For example, Shanghai dispatched hundreds of workers to Tibet to build a wool textile factory in Linzhi, a city in eastern Tibet, during the mid-1960s (Xu 2015).

Even though it was stated by the central government at the end of the 1970s that Tibet would receive assistance from the whole country, in reality, the four provincial level administrative units of Shanghai, Tianjin, Zhejiang, and Sichuan shouldered most, if not all, of the responsibilities of assistance providers to Tibet. Starting from the early 1950s, medical personnel, and teachers were sent to Tibet on a continuous basis as well as materials for the construction of infrastructure. However, it was emphasized that the personnel involved in assistance programs to Tibet should be kept at a relatively small number but they were expected to be of high professional quality (Xu 2015).[3]

Since the reform, the Chinese government has held six conferences specifically to address issues in Tibet. The assistance program for Tibet expanded gradually following each of the conferences that were held, respectively, in 1980, 1984, 1994, 2001, 2010, and 2015. The four administrative units that provided assistance to Tibet based on the decision at the first conference in 1980 were joined by five more cities or provinces from the coastal area based on the decision at the second conference in 1984. These five cities and provinces were Beijing, Jiangsu, Fujian, Shandong, and Guangdong, as is shown in Table 2.2.

A noticeable turning point took place in terms of both the substance and scale of the assistance program in Tibet after the third Tibetan conference in 1994. It was during this meeting that a formal assistance program was designed that reflected the following changes (China News 2014). First, the number of administrative units involved in Tibetan assistance programs grew from nine to fifteen following the conference, which was a significant increase compared with the previous program (Tibet cn 2009). In addition, there seemed to be more efforts to streamline and systematically organize the program, as is reflected in the following program guidelines addressed at the meeting: (The program should emphasize) "specialized responsibilities, participants'

Table 2.2 Tibetan Conferences and Changes of Assistance Partners in Tibet, 1980–2015

Tibetan Conference and Year When It Was Held	*Assistance-Providing Units and Major Changes/Themes*	*Number of Assistance-Providing Units*
First, 1980	Shanghai, Tianjin, Zhejiang, Sichuan	4
Second, 1984	Those since 1st conference, plus Beijing, Jiangsu, Fujian, Shandong, and Guangdong	9
Third, 1994	Those since 2nd conference, plus Chongqing, Hainan, Liaoning, Hunan, Hebei, Shaanxi	15
Fourth, 2001	A ten-year plan (2001–2010) was made and the whole Tibet would receive aid	15
Fifth, 2010	Another ten-year plan (2010–2020) was made and partnership units to commit .01 percent of revenue for the course	17 (nearly all of coastal and central China)
Sixth, 2015	Assistance program was linked to OBOR and other campaigns globally	

Sources: Xu 2015; Tibet, cn 2009; China News 2014; Chinatibetnews 2015.

expertise and specialties, and systematic rotation" (*fenpianfuze, duikouzhiyuan, dingqilunhuan*). It was also decided at the 1994 meeting that there would be a pattern of pairing in the assistance program whereby every two or three municipalities or provinces would be assigned to a specific region or district in Tibet. Furthermore, cadre exchange between Tibet and assistance partner units was to receive greater emphasis in the assistance program. (Beijing Review 1994; Xu 2015).

The change in the content and structure of the assistance program to Tibet during the 1990s reflected the shifting political orientation of ethnic policies in China at the time, following the relatively open and relaxed atmosphere in ethnic minority regions in China during the 1980s. The numerous riots and violent events in both Tibet and Xinjiang starting from the early 1990s led to an enhanced level of political and ideological control in these regions. In addition, student demonstrations in Tiananmen Square in 1989 had most likely also contributed to the change of policies and strict control of religious and cultural activities in Tibet and Xinjiang.

The fourth conference on Tibet, held in 2001, continuously highlighted the importance of cadre assistance, specifically pointing out that more cadre members would be sent from assistance delivering units to Tibet. It was also stated at the meeting that the assistance program, as it had been implemented, would be continued for another 10 years (2001–2010) and that the program would be expanded to include an additional dozen or more counties in Tibet that had not been participants in the program previously. As a result of this latter change, all counties and areas in Tibet would become recipients of the assistance program (China Today 2010).

At the fifth Tibetan conference in 2010, it was announced that a total of RMB 200 billion by the central treasury alone had been devoted to Tibetan assistance programs during the nine years from 2001 to 2010. The huge amount of financial subsidies was said to have resulted in a tremendous success in generating economic gains in Tibet. Consequently, it was stated, the program would continue for another ten-year time frame (2010–2020) with two modifications. One was that the number of participating cities and provinces to provide assistance to Tibet would now be increased to 17, which meant that practically all coastal cities and provinces were participating in the Tibetan assistance program. The other modification was that all the 17 provinces and municipalities were required to commit 0.1 percent of their respective annual financial revenues to the Tibetan assistance program (Xu 2015).

The sixth Tibetan conference, held in 2015 under the Xi administration, connected the Tibetan assistance program to the OBOR campaign in China. Connecting China with South Asia, Tibet is expected to play a significant role in China's expanding global influence. It was also stated that by 2020, Tibetan economy should reach China's average level in terms of residential income (Chinatibetnews 2015).

While official documents in China portray the Tibetan assistance program as highly positive moves in Tibetan social and economic development, scholarly research findings have shown various outcomes of the program. Prior to the intensification of Xinjiang assistance program in 2010, Tibet and adjacent Qinghai Province were the leading recipients of both direct (compensation of budgetary shortfalls by the central government) and indirect (investment by assistance-providing provinces and municipalities) subsidies in economic assistance programs in China (Fischer 2009, 44). Different from other subsidized areas where industrial development and infrastructure construction were usually priorities to receive aid, the assistance to Tibet was overwhelmingly devoted to the tertiary sector of the economy. This is because there was a tremendous amount of financial need for maintenance cost of government administration, which consists of mostly the Han, subsidies for the settlement of the Han population in the region, as well as upkeep expenditure for military and paramilitary sectors in Tibet (Dreyer 2003; Fischer 2009).

Due to the high cost of administrative and military spending and relatively low economic productivity level, governmental subsidies and assistance persistently and significantly surpassed the total GDP value in Tibet (Fischer 2009, 44–46). The following is a quote concerning Tibet's economy and the amount of subsidies it received by a commentator who made the remarks during the mid-1980s:

> Over the previous 30 years, total industrial and agricultural output value increased by four times, while state subsidies increased by 65 times. An increase of one yuan in output value required an increase of 1.21 yuan in state subsidies—i.e. Tibet had a *negative* multiplier effect on investment. (Dreyer 2003, 417)

In other words, economic inefficiency was a serious problem in Tibetan economy facilitated by the assistance program. Furthermore, much of the goods, commodities, and other materials in Tibet are purchased from regions and areas that are providing assistance to Tibet. This results in not only resources being channeled back to the assistance-delivery areas, but also structural and perpetual dependency on subsidies and lack of motivation and/or opportunities for locally centered investment in the economy of Tibet. Furthermore, these economic dynamics also favor state-owned economic sectors and areas populated by the Han, which signifies discrimination against the Tibetan and segregation of the Tibetan population along the lines of, for example, ethnic nationalities and/or urban versus rural sectors (Dreyer 2003; Fischer 2009; Han and Paik 2017).

PARTNERSHIP ASSISTANCE PROGRAM IN XINJIANG

As was discussed earlier, during the initial years of the implementation of assistance programs in China following the National Defense Work Conference in China in 1979, the programs were almost exclusively focused on Tibet. Other administrative units in the western region did not receive nearly as much attention as Tibet had received. Starting from 1979, however, individual coastal provinces or municipalities were matched with Xinjiang to provide aid.[4] A turning point emerged during the meeting of the Polit Bureau Standing Committee of the CCP in March of 1996. Issues concerning Xinjiang were noticeably placed on the agenda of the meeting where the then Party chief of China, Mr. Jiang Zemin, was quoted as having stated the following: (We should) "train and dispatch a large group of Han cadre to work in Xinjiang. These cadre members must adhere to fundamental Party ideologies and orientations, as well as religious and ethnic policies issued by the Party"

(Kunlunwang 2011-09-16). Jiang's statement, together with a document circulated at the meeting titled "Minutes of the Work Meeting of the Party Central Committee on the Stability of Xinjiang," provided the platform to push for large-scale assistance programs in Xinjiang.

The escalating violence that Xinjiang had experienced starting from the early 1990s had most likely been a determining factor in Xinjiang receiving extra attention at the Polit Bureau meeting and subsequently becoming a recipient of a heavy dose assistance. One of the most alarming incidences took place in Baren Township of Akto County of southwestern Xinjiang in 1990 (Hierman 2007). Even though the riot was crushed shortly after it had occurred, it was then followed by a series of additional riots and violence in many parts of Xinjiang (Han and Paik 2017). The declaration of independence of former Soviet territories in Central Asia across from the Xinjiang border and the surge of Islamic movements in the world were an impetus for many in Xinjiang to pursue self-control and independence. The leader of the Baren uprising, for example, was heavily influenced by the idea of "jihad" (holy war) in Afghanistan (Mackerras 2001). In addition, the relatively open atmosphere concerning religious and ethnic issues in China during the 1980s had created space, freedom, and opportunities for many ethnic populations in Xinjiang to engage in cultural and social activities that were deemed significant, such as pilgrimage to Mecca, in order to search for and enhance their ethnic and cultural identity (Primiano 2013). Finally, the increasing gap between the coastal and western regions in terms of socioeconomic development in China, as well as the socioeconomic disparities between the Han and minorities in Xinjiang (Hannum and Xie 1998; Heilig 2006), led to resentment and disillusionment among many ethnic minority populations, who were left behind in benefiting from China's huge economic gains. All these factors helped explain the contentious situation in Xinjiang that led to much more turbulence and frequent violence during the 1990s compared with any time in the PRC era up until that time. The violence took many forms ranging from riots and protests, to bombings, arsons, and assassinations (Hierman 2007).

Following Jiang's comments, the initial campaign to provide assistance to Xinjiang consisted of nearly exclusive dispatch of Han cadre and professionals from various parts of eastern China. The rationale for these efforts was obvious: The instability in Xinjiang was perceived as symptomatic of a lack of integration between Xinjiang and the rest of China. As Jiang stated in his speech in 1996, messages must be delivered to Xinjiang about the importance of ethnic minority areas adhering to Party ideologies and orientations and being loyal to and integrated with the motherland. To accomplish this mission, a large number of messengers, typically cadre members and other professionals from coastal and inland areas, were perceived to be needed in Xinjiang.

In February 1997, shortly after the Polit Bureau meeting, more than 200 administrators and professionals arrived in Xinjiang representing the following provinces and municipalities: Beijing, Tianjin, Shanghai, Shandong, Jiangsu, Zhejiang, Jiangxi, Henan, and Hebei, as well as selected departments at the state level. Shortly afterwards, additional provinces, including Guangdong, Liaoning, Fujian, Hunan, and Hubei, started sending cadre to Xinjiang as well (Chen 2013). As a result, fourteen provinces and municipalities were involved in providing cadre assistance to Xinjiang. By the end of 2004, a total of 1,700 individuals were sent to the region (Yaxin 2010). This number more than doubled by 2010 when the accumulated number of assistant personnel reached 3,749 (Qiao 2010).

Thanks to the nearly exclusive emphasis on the aspect of personnel assistance, the Xinjiang assistance program during the 1990s was simply referred to as programs of cadre assistance in Xinjiang (Qiao 2010). This situation lasted for nearly ten years before a more comprehensive approach was adopted for the assistance program. In 2005 the central government decided to modify the assistance programs for Xinjiang by sending to the region not only cadre members, but also material goods and commodities, financial resources and technical support for assisting Xinjiang's economic development. The initial economic support packages, however, were only delivered to four specifically designated districts and prefectures in southern Xinjiang (i.e., Hotan, Kashgar, Aksu, and Kizilsu), as well as the three Bingtuan divisions stationed in these areas (Division 3 in Kashgar, Division 14 in Hotan, and Division 1 in Aksu).[5] Furthermore, much of the economic support was expected to be facilitated by state-controlled key industrial companies and businesses such as China Yangtze River Three Gorges Project Development Corporation (中国长江三峡工程开发总公司) (Yang 2010).

Meanwhile, in dealing with escalating and increasingly widespread tension in Xinjiang, the government adopted a "strike hard" policy, reversing the milder approach during the previous decade. The situation became even more tense after the September 11 incidence that led to the global war on terror and Muslim fundamentalism championed by the United States. These events and movements at the international level had a particularly strong impact on Xinjiang where wars were launched against what the Chinese government termed three "evils"— the evils of "separatism," "fundamentalism," and "terrorism." With the assumption that the three types of evil forces were all interconnected, the Chinese government engaged intensive campaigns in both domestic policies and foreign diplomacy as part of the three anti-ism efforts. Through diplomatic maneuvering and involvement in multinational organizations such as Shanghai Five (later renamed Shanghai Corporation Organization (SCO)), China successfully gained support from countries across from Xinjiang's border to be aligned with the Chinese government in its efforts to suppress activities that were deemed as threatening to the stability of the country. For example, under pressure from China, nearly all Central Asian countries banned political rallies and military training by Uyghur dissidents in their territories (Millward 2007). At the domestic level, the central government sped up the pace to develop the western part of China. The GWDS, which was launched at the end of the last century and is still ongoing, is arguably the most large-scale campaign that the PRC government has implemented in developing China's western region, including Xinjiang, as was discussed above.

The central government of China revised the assistance program for Xinjiang again in 2007. Based on a document concerning Xinjiang's social and economic development, it was announced that the Xinjiang assistance program would be expanded in terms of both geographic territories that would be covered by the program and the comprehensiveness of the program.[6] All of Xinjiang, instead of just selected areas in southern part of the region, would become aid recipients and the assistance programs would cover a wider range of subject areas including technological and economic support and education, health care and other social welfare areas (Yang 2010). In terms of the scope of the assistance, not only economic and material resources, but higher education and technological support would be emphasized as well (Chen 2013). Of course, personnel, or cadre, assistance would still remain one of the key components, if not the key component, of the assistance packages.

The Xinjiang assistance program experienced the most significant milestone change in 2010 following the first Conference on Xinjiang Assistance Program in March and Xinjiang Work Conference in May of that year. In light of the magnitude of the damage and seriousness and the violent nature of the July 2009 Urumqi riot, the central government of China revisited once again the assistance program and made it the centerpiece of policies to stimulate the economy and reduce ethnic tensions in Xinjiang. A comprehensive blueprint was announced concerning the most recent version of the Xinjiang assistance program. Retaining the existing structure, the 2010 version of the program reflected the following additions and changes:

1. The provinces of Anhui, Shanxi, Heilongjiang, and Jilin, the only four provinces in non-western China that had not been directly involved in the Xinjiang assistance program until then, as well as the city of Shenzhen in southern China, which is one of the most economically affluent cities in China, became the latest participants in the Xinjiang assistance program (News SINA 2010.05.04). This means that nearly all provinces and major municipalities in the coastal and central regions of China had joined the team of Xinjiang assistance programs.[7]
2. A set amount of financial assistance (0.3 to 0.6 percent of the fiscal revenue of the assistance-providing provinces or cities) is required to be

devoted to the Xinjiang assistance program by all participating administrative units (China Daily May 21, 2010).

3. A ten-year time span (2011–2020) was planned for the program, which could potentially be extended if the central government deems it necessary to do so. By 2020, Xinjiang is projected to be built into a moderately prosperous society (*xiaokang shehui*) with the help of the aid through the assistance program (Baiduwenku 2010).
4. With personnel or cadre assistance remaining as the cornerstone element, social welfare, and economic development are also said to be significant components of the program.
5. The dispatch of cadre and professionals, arguably the most challenging aspect of the assistance program, has now become an institutionalized practice with guidelines and stipulations in order to entice participation in the program. Some of the guidelines were established by the central government, but local administrative units also produced details to ensure the smooth operation of the program, as is discussed in chapter 4.

With the major facelift, the Xinjiang assistance program has been in full swing. Five more conferences on Xinjiang assistance program have been held since the first conference in 2010. This means a pattern of almost an annual meeting organized by the central government on this issue. The most recent meeting, the sixth one, took place in Kashgar in 2017. In addition to avowing to continue the existing models of the program, it was stated at the meeting that the program would adapt to the "new concept, new ideas and new strategy" (新理念新思想新战略) of the Xi administration's approach of governing the country (Xinhuanet 2017). This means that the OBOR campaign and the efforts to realize the "China Dream," both initiatives of the Xi-Li administration, would have a major impact on the Xinjiang assistance program.

SUMMARY

The PRC produced perhaps the first official policies on ethnic relations and ethnic minority populations in China. According to these policies, it is the legal and moral responsibility for Han-dominant areas in China to provide aid to ethnic minority regions. When, how, in what amount and format, and to what extent the aid is to be provided, however, is totally determined by what the Chinese government perceives to be the most pressing issues in China as a whole. It is, in other words, for the sake of enhancing the national interest and nation-building that the assistance programs have been carried out, as the cases of both Tibet and Xinjiang have illustrated.

The assistance program that has been implemented in Xinjiang since 2010 is no exception to this general rule. If there is a difference, it is that the recent wave of the Xinjiang assistance program is much more formal and structured and has been practically made into a long-term national movement participated by virtually all administrative units in coastal and central regions. The huge economic gains that these regions have achieved since the reform have not only helped sustain the program financially, but provide and enhance conceptual frameworks to justify the aggressive implementation of the assistance program in Xinjiang. The next chapter will analyze these theoretical frameworks.

NOTES

1. GWDS is a campaign that the Chinese government started at the end of the 20th century under the administration of Jiang Zemin and Zhu Rongji. The campaign emphasizes the construction of infrastructure in western China and is one of the most costly government-initiated projects in PRC. It has also generated tremendous controversy over issues such as the style of implementation, the process of decision-making and the effectiveness of the intended achievement of the program (guoqing.china.com.cn 2012; Holbig 2004; Goodman 2004; Han and Paik 2017).
2. After taking over Tibet in 1950, the CCP established its rule in the region based on a 17-point agreement signed by both the Tibetan (reluctantly, according some sources (e.g., Crowe 2013)) and the Chinese governments. But the agreement was later repudiated by the Tibetan leader, the 14th Dalai Lama, during the 1959 uprising when he fled Tibet and established a Tibetan government-in-exile in Dharamsala of northern India. The Chinese government subsequently engaged in political, economic, and social reforms in Tibet. Assistance programs have since been an integral part of PRC's policy implementations in the region.
3. One of the reasons for not sending a large number of people to Tibet was probably the fear of resentment from the Tibetan population and reaction from international communities concerning the influx of a large number of Han population into the region (Dreyer 2003).
4. One researcher points out that the coastal province of Jiangsu was asked to provide financial assistance to Xinjiang as early as 1979. Shanghai became another assistance deliverer in 1984, followed by Shandong in 1996 (Chen 2013).
5. (1) As was discussed in the previous chapter, southern Xinjiang is predominantly inhabited by minority populations and is among the most economically underdeveloped areas in China. (2) The term "division" refers to the units of XPCG or *Bingtuan.*
6. In September 2007, the State Department of China produced a document titled "Suggestions by the State Council concerning the Further Stimulation of the Economic and Social Development of Xinjiang" (国务院关于进一步促进新疆经济社会发展的若干意见). It was stated in the

document that by 2010, Xinjiang's economy was projected to reach the national average level. The document also points out that by 2020, Xinjiang would become one of the emerging sites of rapid economic growth in the western region of the country, realizing the goal of a moderately prosperous society (*xiaokang shehui*). In addition, it would play a major role in China's further opening up to the outside world (xjkunlun 2013).

7. The only administrative unit in the coastal and central China that is not included in the Xinjiang assistance program is Hainan Province, which is an island in southern China and the smallest province in China. It was formerly part of Guangdong Province and was designated as a separate province in 1988.

Chapter 3

Theoretical Perspectives on Interventional Programs

The assistance program in Xinjiang has been presented by the central government of China as a strategically important move in the development of the national economy and maintenance of social security and stability. Even though the program demands a tremendous amount of commitment and sacrifice in terms of financial, human capital, technological, and other resources by coastal and central regions of China, these areas and regions seem to be willing to accept the rationale and justification for this program, as will be demonstrated in the following chapters. It is difficult, however, to assess the sentiment at the receiving end of the program, especially of the ethnic minority populations in Xinjiang.[1] Based on the large body of literature concerning minority populations' deep resentment of many of PRC policies in Xinjiang, it is safe to assume that the assistance program is probably not as welcomed by ethnic minority populations as the government would like to project.

How did the Chinese government persuade those who have to provide the aid to actively participate in the program? How is the assistance program justified and articulated to local populations in Xinjiang? How should the assistance program be conceptualized in terms of its background, strategy, rationale, implementation, and outcome from a scholarly viewpoint? Finally, how consistent are official statements and scholarly discussions concerning this heavily interventional program? In this chapter, I will first review relevant scholarly discussions on interventional programs in many parts of the world and then analyze both official and scholarly presentations in China to justify the most recent wave of the Xinjiang assistance program. These discussions should provide us with conceptual tools to understand the rationale and implementation strategies of the program as well as to predict future outcomes of the Xinjiang assistance program.

ASSISTANCE PROGRAM AND UTOPIAN IDEOLOGY

As was discussed in the previous chapter, assistance programs implemented in Xinjiang and other areas of China since the early years of the PRC have been consistently employed as intervening measures to help achieve goals and objectives set by the Chinese government, which include, among other things, the enhancement of the Party ideology, the strengthening of the control of ethnic minority areas, the stimulation of the national economy, and the expansion of China's influences globally. In other words, the assistance program is portrayed to have the capacity to help enhance the well-being of the nation and move the country to an improved and more desirable status. Since there are disparities in terms of the distance to the envisioned destination among the various populations, cultures, communities, and regions, as well as varied levels of capabilities of reaching the perceived goal, those who fall behind would need help and assistance in the journey. The variations of geographic locations and populations in their status and capabilities of realizing goals outlined by the authorities, in other words, are viewed as problematic and must be corrected. The assistance program has been pursued as an effective remedy in solving this problem, at least as it is perceived by the central government.

Clearly, the root cause of the idea of the assistance program is the assumption that China is making strides toward some kind of futuristic environment that promises to be a significant improvement in terms of overall societal well-being compared with the past and current situations. According to this perspective, the existing societal conditions are viewed as inadequate, deficient, backward, or antiquated and therefore they must be improved, upgraded, or abandoned. This is particularly the case in periphery areas where special assistance must be provided to help facilitate the expected changes.

China is not alone in pursuing a utopian society and presuming the tendency for human populations to strive to improve their social and environmental circumstances. Utopianist viewpoints have been reflected in countless institutional establishments and social movements throughout history and across a wide range of cultural contexts. Unfortunately, as researchers point out, these attempts have rarely achieved the expected outcomes. On the contrary, they are often proven to be failed experiments and have generated disastrous consequences to both the social and physical environment (Gray 2007, Scott 1998). For example, utopianist ideologies have been used as justifications by religious movements to carry out "sacred" missions to rescue human species but they often result in violence and destruction; by political dictators to engage in organizational behaviors for the expected collective good, which frequently produce atrocious measures to "legitimately" bring torture and death to countless innocent people; and by bureaucratic governments to implement policies and programs that, albeit sometimes with good intentions, often end up generating catastrophic consequences and suffering and misery to massive numbers of ordinary citizens (Gray 2007).

Marxism is arguably the most influential force behind the widespread and turbulent revolutionary movements to pursue the ultimate utopian society by establishing communism across the world in modern history. Consistent with numerous other societies that practiced Marxism, the PRC has mobilized a tremendous amount of resources and engaged in large-scale and fundamental institutional changes in the construction of socialism in order to pave the way for the realization of utopian communism. After three decades of vigorous and dogmatic adherence to Marxist ideologies from 1949 when the PRC was founded until the late 1970s, however, policy makers of China decided to engage in the market reform in the country.

CHINA'S REFORM AND UTOPIAN IDEOLOGY

Immediately following the passing of the earliest founders of the PRC, the second generation of leaders, headed by Mr. Deng Xiaoping, made the bold decision to introduce market forces to and start the economic reform in China at the end of the 1970s. Opening its doors to lure foreign investment, encouraging private entrepreneurship, and advocating market competition and free enterprises, China appeared to have abandoned the Marxist and socialist principles on which the CCP had been established and according to which the Party had been operating for decades.

Despite the many drastic changes in the economic and social institutions as a result of the reform, post-reform China has still maintained many aspects of political and economic arrangements based on Marxist convictions. For example, it still adheres to the one party (the CCP) rule as well as the dominance of state ownership. As a matter of fact, the series of CCP leaders since the reform have consistently stressed the point that China is a socialist country and that the reform is simply an alternative approach to stimulate the economy and enhance the collective well-being of the people in China. In the words of China's official stance, the reform is intended for China to "develop socialism with Chinese characteristics."[2]

It is perhaps debatable whether China under the reform is still a socialist country (Han 2006; Wang, X. 2016). But what is clear is the consistency of the utopian nature of the assumption of social changes both before and after the reform. Social arrangements inspired by the prospect of a brighter future and an improved social environment have served as guiding principles in both time periods. On the other hand, there does seem to be a not-so-subtle difference in the official rhetoric to define the two types of utopian societies before and after the reform. While the prospect of communism, an ambiguous and abstract notion, served as the driving force of socialist construction in pre-reform PRC, the reform since the end of the 1970s is viewed as being the most effective measure to enable China to enter a stage of a moderately prosperous society (*xiaokang shehui*) within a foreseeable future. In other words, compared with earlier propaganda that tended to be vague and extremely idealistic, the slogan during the reform period has a much more subdued and moderate and yet realistic tone, demonstrating a more pragmatic attitude and approach of post-reform Chinese leadership compared with the founders of the PRC.

In addition to rhetoric statements in political discussions, the more pragmatic and rational approach to reform is also reflected in the overwhelming emphasis on the development of science and technology and on programs and policies with rational and practical purposes. Realizing that there is a huge gap between China and the western societies (and Japan) in terms of technological and scientific development and attributing it to the comparatively less developed status of China's industrialization and modernization, Chinese leaders, with significant input from academia, are determined to make up for the inadequacies (Wang, H. 2007). A huge amount of resources have been devoted to scientific research, technological development, training of scientists and technical personnel, and construction and development of scientific institutions and infrastructure (Schweinberger 2014). Halper compares resources devoted to technological development between "traditional powerhouses for technological development" and China by stating:

> In an arresting statistic, we find that R&D in the United States and Europe grew by 1–2 percent between 2001 and 2006, while figures for the same period in China increased by 26 percent. Since 1996, America's overall expenditures on R&D in computers and office equipment fell by over one-third, while expenditures in China rose by 47 percent. (Helper 2012, 41–42)

In other words, not only has China set more moderate and practical goals to achieve technological progress, but it has also adopted more utilitarian and positivist-oriented strategies in achieving the goals. The realistic orientation is also reflected in other strategies to stimulate the economy, including the encouragement of private and township industries and entrepreneurship as well as foreign investment, flexible intervention by the government in the economy, and a mix of market forces and governmental control in guiding the reform. In sum, following the advice of its leader Deng Xiaoping, China adopted an approach of "crossing a river by groping for the stone" to guide the reform, meaning the reform proceeded in a very cautious and experimental way (Wang, X. 2016).

There is little doubt that the pragmatic outlook and rational and flexible approach are significant contributing factors to the huge success of China's reform, especially evaluated in economic terms. The consistently high economic growth rate of double or close to double-digit figures over the last several decades in China is considered a miracle in the modern history of economic development in the world. "Between 2000 and 2010, China's GDP increased five-fold from $1.2 trillion to $5.9 trillion, and its foreign-exchange reserves increased 17-fold from $165 billion to over $2.8 trillion" (Wyne 2011, 6). Thanks to its remarkable economic performance, China reached the milestone of becoming the world's second largest economy in 2011 and some argue that it would soon surpass the United States and become the largest economy in the world (Subramanian 2011).[3]

Not surprisingly, the Chinese government takes great pride in the remarkable economic performance and technological development of China since the reform, appearing confidently assured that China is moving increasingly closer to the goal of becoming a moderately prosperous society. This type of excitement has been frequently expressed in the mass media. A presentation, for example, produced by *Economic Daily*, a Chinese official publication, at the beginning of 2017, has been widely circulated on the internet to boast China's economic and technological achievements. The program starts with the demonstration of the rapid development of space industries in China in recent years, most noticeably the successful launching of numerous satellites, rockets, and other spacecrafts. It then goes on to point out that China takes the lead in the world in many scientific innovations and technological accomplishments. For example, China is said to rank number one in the world among a long list of innovations and accomplishments including the total length of highway, high-speed rail, and interior water transportation; the total number of bridges; the total volume of cargo and container goods processed annually as well as regular and express package deliveries; the number of tunnels and bridges with the highest physical elevations as well as the most difficult conditions under which they are built; the cable-stayed bridge with the most dramatic angle, which means the construction process of the highest degree of complexity and technical difficulties; and, last but by no means least, the highest speed computers. Viewers of the program are also frequently reminded that all these achievements have been obtained within merely several decades since the reform (Southcn.com 2017-02-04).

SCHOLARLY DISCUSSIONS ON CHINA'S REFORM ACHIEVEMENT

China's remarkable performance in economic and technological development has generated much scholarly research both inside and outside of China (e.g., Han 2006; Halper 2012; Jacques 2009; Liu 2010; Miller 2017). Seen as the leading force to guide the movement toward modernization and an advanced social order, China's experience promises to offer an alternative model to traditional western capitalism. Different from the neoliberal model of free-market fundamentalist capitalism, some researchers argue, China has developed its own state-coordinated capitalist system and has achieved remarkable success at least measured in terms of economic development (Schweinberger 2014). Referred to as "state capitalism" or "Sino-capitalism," China's development model is based on the combined forces of the mighty state power and the huge amount of economic resources to control, stimulate, and develop the economy.

With China at the forefront of economies that share similar experiences in their developmental approach, including Brazil, Russia, and India (i.e., the BRIC), the term "Beijing consensus" is used by some to refer to the ideological basis of the type of capitalist models practiced by these countries. It is said to be in competition with or even replacing the "Washington consensus," the model of market capitalism that had dominated the global capitalist order until the rise of the BRICs, particularly after the global economic crisis of 2008 (McNally 2005, 743, 2013). For example, when China initiated the founding of the Asian Infrastructure Investment Bank (AIIB) in 2013 as an alternative to established financial institutions controlled by western capitalist countries, it was resisted vehemently by the United States which appealed to many of its allies not to join the institution. The overwhelmingly enthusiastic participation in the institution with a membership of scores of countries, including many American allies, however, "stunned" all parties involved, including even China herself (Perlez 2015).

Other researchers credit China for its strategies of focusing on economic development without being sidetracked by political or other controversial issues. By avoiding conflict and interference with affairs of foreign countries, China has been successfully expanding its influence and bringing peace and harmony while investing in not only its own economy but also that of many other countries (Jacques 2009; Kang 2007).

Furthermore, some researchers, particularly those in China, assertively establish a causal relationship between the CCP ideologies and China's economic achievements. Several high-profile academics have been giving presentations to raise nationalist sentiment, particularly among young people, in China. The social media has again been frequently utilized as an effective media source for this end. The following are two examples:

Professor Jin Yinan at the National Defense University of China has given numerous presentations to promote the CCP influence in China's economic success. One of the most well-known presentations is titled "From a Hundred Years of Vicissitude to the Rise of a Great Nation, from a Sick Man in East Asia to National Rejuvenation." Focusing on changes that occurred in China during the entire 20th century, Jin argues that China experienced waves of reform efforts at the beginning of the 20th century, but none of them was successful. It was ultimately the CCP that has fundamentally transformed China from a weak state repeatedly bullied by western imperialist countries to an independent and powerful nation. The CCP made this transformation a success by adhering to the practice of Marxism. More importantly, the CCP has made necessary adjustments and changes to Marxist theory to fit the unique circumstances of China. In conclusion, Jin made the statement "Marxism changed China and China changed Marxism," which brought a burst of applause from the audience who were mostly, if not all, university students.[4]

Specifically, Jin continues, by establishing the PRC in 1949, the CCP enhanced the political power of Chinese people in an unprecedentedly significant and meaningful way. By winning the Korean War during the 1950s, the CCP elevated China's military status to a qualitatively more advanced level. Then, by engaging in the economic reform toward the end of the 20th century, the CCP has realized the long-cherished dream of building a strong economy and a powerful Chinese nation. Of all the profound changes that took place in China during the second half of the last century, Jin concludes, the most important is the significant increase of collective consciousness and a sense of nationalism among the Chinese people (Kunlunce.com 2017-01-04).

Another academic whose work to foster patriotism in China has been widely circulated is Professor Ma Shizhuang at the University of the Chinese Academy of Sciences (UCAS). His speech "A Mao Zedong Appeared in China" was delivered as a part of a lecture series titled "Practice and Research on the Theory of Socialism with Chinese Characteristics" at UCAS. Rehearsing throughout his talk the political rhetoric of Mao being a great military leader, a smart economist, a wise politician, a brilliant historian, an insightful philosopher, a fluent poet, an excellent calligrapher, and so on, Ma nonetheless managed to raise interest, enthusiasm, and probably a great degree of resonance of his students. He achieved this by connecting Mao's era at the beginning of the last century with lives of students during the contemporary time period. For example, Ma comments that just like college students during the 21st century, Mao and his peers a hundred years ago also faced the difficult choice and dilemma between whether to attend educational institutions in western countries or stay in China, whether to try to advance a professional career or pursue a more meaningful goal in life, and whether to focus on taking care of his family and personal affairs or engage in social movements to transform China. Mao's ultimate decision and his commitment to the course of the CCP played an essential role in fundamentally changing China from a weak and feudalist society tormented by war, chaos, famine, and other disasters and miseries to an independent nation with political dignity, national pride, and economic advancement.

Since, following the logic of the arguments by these academics, Marxism and Maoism have played such an important role in leading China on the progressively forward and upward path, China should, of course, continue the journey guided by the CCP that avows to persistently observe Marxist principles. In addition, as China's leaders and academics argue, the CCP should not limit itself for progress and improvement for the people of China only. It is China's responsibility as one of the most powerful nations and strongest economies in the globalized world to extend its experience, resources, and knowhow to other parts of the world. As Professor Jin comments, "We should not be overly content just because we have been fairly successful thus far or because we have legacies to share with the world such as the panda, the Confucius influences, the Chinese cuisine and so on. We need to keep up with the expectations of the changing world and keep making progress. We must come up with new agendas and programs to meet the challenge of leading the world forward" (Tengxunshipin 2017).

SCHOLARLY DISCUSSION ON SOCIAL PROBLEMS IN POST-REFORM CHINA

It is against such a backdrop that China has been aggressively launching programs for economic and technological development not only within China but also in many parts of the world. The most recent high-profile program that China has been involved in is the One-Belt One-Road (OBOR) initiative officially started by China's administration in 2013. The OBOR project proposes to construct a network of infrastructure, industrial, transportation, and communication facilities along the ancient Silk Road to develop huge economic corridors that would connect China with Central Asia, southeast Asia, northern Africa, and ultimately Europe. Based on the face value, it seems highly likely that the OBOR initiative could be a mechanism to equalize the distribution of socioeconomic resources in the world as it would help bring benefits of global industrialization to a large portion of the world's population, including many in some of the most impoverished regions.[5] When viewed this way, China and the CCP seem to be indeed playing an active role in improving the well-being of the world's populations.

Paradoxically, however, studies have repeatedly demonstrated that post-reform China itself is one of the most severely stratified countries in the world measured in terms of income and wealth distribution such as Gini coefficient (Whyte 2016; Xie and Zhou 2014). Some studies show that due to the continuous rise of income inequality since the 1980s, China has become the single most unequal country in the world (Creed and Liu 2014; Whyte 2016). Furthermore, the economic polarization in China is a relatively recent but rapidly growing phenomenon. Prior to the reform, China was a model in the world for egalitarianism in terms of social and economic welfare. Indeed, the change from a model of egalitarianism to an extremely stratified society is one of the most severe and unfortunate setbacks that have taken place in China, according to sociological perspectives (Wilkinson and Pickett 2009).

The socioeconomic stratification in China, as severe as it is, is nonetheless not even among the most aggravating problems that Chinese people find troublesome. One author, based on his research in China over the last several decades, points out that China is ridden with a host of other problems that have resulted from the reform and economic advancement and that Chinese people have been found to be most angry about. The author presents the following list, which is by no means exhaustive, to illustrate the multitude and seriousness of such problems: "shady deals by officials to confiscate farmland and urban housing, diversion of public resources for official enrichment, local governments' failures to protect the public from toxic chemical spills and adulterated food products, coercive enforcement of family planning, crackdowns on religion, and incarceration of critics of official abuses" (Whyte 2016, 36). Another author lists what he refers to as "side effects" of China's "miracle growth": "endemic corruption, environmental crisis, income inequality, displaced populations, extreme poverty, an urban-rural divide, inflation, an angry nationalist youth, endemic work-related health problems, and heavy restrictions on the media" (Halper 2010, 43).

Martin Whyte makes an analogy between the ferocious nature of these social problems and the levels of violence and destruction of volcano eruption and argues that the consequences of these and other social injustices and malpractices in China could potentially be so catastrophic that it is a matter of time before these dormant volcanoes become active in spite of the huge economic gains that China has experienced (Whyte 2016).[6]

CHINA'S ETHNIC POLICIES, ETHNIC TENSION, AND ASSISTANCE PROGRAMS

Arguably the most challenging problem with the most far-reaching and detrimental consequences that China faces is racial tension and conflict (Hao and Liu 2012; Halper 2012; Sun 2014). China is a relatively homogeneous nation with eight percent of its population being officially classified as ethnic minorities. But the distribution of China's ethnic populations is closely associated with patterns of geographic, social, and economic characteristics. While the Han population concentrates in the eastern part of China, minority populations are spread across at least half of China's geographic territories in the west, with some of the provinces and regions, such as Tibet in the far west and Xinjiang in the northwestern corner, predominantly inhabited by ethnic minorities. The relationship between China proper and these remote minority regions has been marked with turbulent patterns of interaction and sentiments of negativity, hostility, and animosity in the thousands of years of Chinese history.

The two Chinese characters referring to China literally mean "middle kingdom (*zhongguo*)." It suggests a taken-for-granted mentality of the central and significant position of China in relation to the periphery status of peoples and territories at the outskirts of the middle kingdom. Located on the flat land mass north of the Yangtze River, the ancient "middle kingdom" was surrounded by diverse geographic typologies: It faced the ocean to the east, deep jungles to the south, large stretches of deserts to the north, and huge mountain ranges to the west. Consequently, economic and cultural patterns in the "middle kingdom" were in sharp contrast with those in periphery areas thanks to the drastically different ecological, environmental, and climatic features. While the middle kingdom prided itself for its rich culture with settled farming and sophisticated cities and governing institutions, the periphery populations were either nomadic drifters living an unsettled life on horses' back or tribe dwellers living off of jungles who were all viewed as barbarous and uncivilized (Dreyer 1976; Harrell 1990, 1997 (a) and (b); McKhann 1997; Pan 1992).

With the gradual assimilation of ethnic populations adjacent to the core territories of the middle kingdom over the centuries, the demarcation dividing the core and periphery regions have been pushed further and further away from the core area. This gradual geographic and physical recession of outer regions as a result of annexation of these territories by China over the centuries only promoted even more intensely a prejudicial and negative attitude of the Han Chinese toward the distant territories and unfamiliar populations (Sun 2014).

The paternalistic and chauvinistic attitude of the Han-superiority that has been part of legacies of Chinese culture for thousands of years has had a strong impact on PRC policies and practices concerning ethnic relations. The pursuit of a Marxist utopian social order that envisioned global emancipation and universally based egalitarianism should, at least in theory, have helped reduce interethnic tension and stratification. This is because Marxism emphasizes the need for people of all ethnicities and nationalities to work together as one working class toward the ultimate goal of a communist utopian society. In practice, however, it has been proven to be difficult for the CCP to bring solidarity and integration to all PRC ethnic groups due to, among other things, the disagreement between the Party and ethnic minorities in terms of the extent to which autonomy be granted to the latter.

As was pointed out in chapter 1, the PRC produced the first official documents and policies in the long history of China for ethnic relations and the treatment of ethnic minority populations. Overturning earlier suppositions that ethnic minority populations and territories would be permitted to have complete self-determination and secede from the middle kingdom if they would be so inclined,[7] the PRC ethnic minority policies agreed only to a limited degree of autonomy for the ethnic minority population (Gladney 2004). Besides, it is confined to the areas of language, culture, and economics. Ethnic minorities' seceding from China was no longer considered a possibility.

To gain genuine autonomy, however, has been a cherished goal for minority populations in China, especially the Tibetan and Uyghur, as well as countless ethnic populations around the world. Indeed, the yearning for establishing ethnic and cultural identity and receiving autonomous status by ethnic groups is a major force that has led to countless conflicts and wars in the world since ancient times (Li and Niemann 2016; Riphenburg 2005; Sekulic 2004). One of the concepts scholars use to explain this phenomenon is primordialism, which refers to individuals' natural and inborn features, such as ancestry, language, religion, and custom, as well as a certain degree of obligations, loyalties, and devotions expected of group members to their ethnic and religious communities (Gusfield 1996; Harrell 1997 (a) and (b); Sekulic 2004). Similar to the experiences of ethnic populations in other parts of the world, these primordial characteristics have played fundamental roles in Uyghur peoples' repeated demonstrations to preserve their cultural identities and heritages during the PRC era (Davis 2008; Hierman 2007).

The Chinese government has used both sticks, including ruthless suppressions, and carrots, such as assistance programs, in dealing with the ensuing racial tension. By delivering materials, technology, financial aids, social welfare, and ideological indoctrinations, all of which are presumed to help facilitate the stability, stimulate economic development, and raise the living standard in ethnic minority areas, the government obviously expects a more appeased populace in these areas.

SUMMARY

The assistance program is a heavily interventional approach to facilitate the application of the utopian ideology that human conditions could and should be progressively improved. This viewpoint has guided many movements in world history to alter human societies, including China's campaigns for socialist construction. The economic success of China's reform has only helped reinforce the influence of this perspective.

There are, however, opposing viewpoints concerning using intervening programs to bring so-called progress to human societies. John Gray is one of the most eloquent representatives of this line of arguments, as he states:

> Believers in progress – . . . – think of ethics and politics as being like science, with each step forward enabling further advances in future. Improvement in society is cumulative, they believe, so that the elimination of one evil can be followed by the removal of others in an open-ended process. But human affairs show no sign of being additive in this way: what is gained can always be lost, sometimes – . . . – in a blink of an eye. Human knowledge tends to increase, but humans do not become any more civilized as a result. They remain prone to every kind of barbarism, and while the growth of knowledge allows them to improve their material conditions, it also increases the savagery of their conflicts. (Gray 2007, 187–188)

The assistance program in China is such an interventional project that is designed to achieve perceived improvement in social environment. It started as irregular moves of sending materials and other necessities deemed to be needed in remote frontier regions during the early years of the PRC. It has become increasingly more comprehensive, formal, and institutionalized with the most recent campaign starting in 2010 and still unfolding in Xinjiang. As will be demonstrated in the following chapters, the assistance program is drastically altering Xinjiang's cultural, economic, geographic, and demographic landscapes but with the long-term consequence being difficult to predict.

NOTES

1. One of the major reasons for the difficulties is that it is not easy to conduct research in Xinjiang on topics that are deemed sensitive by the government (Caprioni 2012; Rudelson 1998; Yee 2005).

2. The speech delivered by Mr. Hu Jintao, the party chief of the CCP from 2003 to 2013, at the 18th CCP national congress on November 8, 2012, was titled "March forward without Astray along the Road of Socialism Construction with Chinese Characteristics and Strive to Build a Comprehensive Moderately Prosperous Society" (*jiandingbuyi yanzhe zhongguotese shehuizhuyi daolu qianjin, wei quanmian jiancheng xiaokang shehui er fendou* (cpc.people.com 2012).

3. This speculation has been challenged by researchers (Carter 2014).

4. Jin's statement is apparently a reiteration of the concept of "socialism with Chinese characteristics."

5. This is argued to be yet another area in which China's state capitalist model is different from the western capitalist development model. The latter, at least at the beginning of its development, benefited only the elite members of its own population.

6. The real dilemma, according to Whyte, is that the problems persist in spite of waves of campaigns that China has launched to ease public outcry. Unless the Chinese government is willing to consider fundamental structural changes and institutional rearrangements, argues Whyte, China is just not in the position to fundamentally tackle these problems.

7. It was articulated in the Jiangxi Constitution in 1931 that the CCP was for "the right of self-determination of the national minorities in China, the right to a complete separation from China, and the right of each national minority to form an independent state" (Hsieh 1986, 6).

Chapter 4

Cadre and Personnel Assistance to Xinjiang

Cadre is an ambiguous concept that is not easy to operationalize, but it is extremely important in PRC's political, social, and economic stratification systems. Among all occupational categories in the PRC, cadres are the most privileged with relatively high income, prestige and social status, and better benefits and welfare compared with other employment categories. There is an organizational structure of hierarchy according to which cadre members are ranked and their salary, benefit, and access to various resources are determined. Almost all governmental officials and a large proportion of civil service personnel in China are cadres, so are administrators at various state and public companies and organizations such as education, health care, and social services institutions.[1]

As was mentioned earlier, the cadre assistance has consistently been the cornerstone of assistance programs to Xinjiang. As a matter of fact, during the first decade after the institutionalization of the assistance program (1996–2005), the assistance program in Xinjiang comprised of almost exclusively cadre and personnel assistance. The reason for this, as was discussed in chapter 2, was because of the escalating ethnic conflicts that Xinjiang had experienced starting from the early 1990s. The exclusive focus on cadre assistance was apparently an intended measure to cope with the racial tension and social instability in the region. Cadre members were sent to Xinjiang to help quell the unrest and, more importantly, participate in the CCP ideological indoctrination.[2]

In order to understand the comprehensiveness, complexity, and subtlety of the phenomenon of cadre assistance, we need to review historical patterns of efforts made by the Chinese government during various time periods to dispatch individuals to Xinjiang. These individuals included governmental officials, civilians, military personnel, and criminals who had to make the

Xinjiang-bound journey under a wide range of conditions. The experience of these people's involuntary migration is a telling point in the analysis of Xinjiang's periphery status, both physically and culturally, and the Chinese government's policies toward Xinjiang.

HISTORICAL PATTERNS OF DISPATCHING OFFICIAL AND SOCIAL UNDESIRABLES TO XINJIANG

The practice of sending governmental officials, civil service personnel, and other individuals to remote places like Xinjiang is nothing new in China. During historical times, officials, and civilians were sent to Xinjiang for drastically different reasons. While some were dispatched there to perform administrative duties, many others found themselves in Xinjiang because they had been impeached or convicted of criminal behavior. For at least the last two millennia, Chinese governments have recurrently sent disgraced governmental officials, together with many other types of convicted criminals or offenders, to frontier areas where the convicts served their sentences (Seymour and Anderson 1998, 12). Criminals and those who were viewed as "trouble makers" were often treated as slaves or "military exiles" (*chongjun*) (Seymour and Anderson 1998, 12–13). This large pool of free or cheap labor of both civilian and military personnel undoubtedly helped the government to build a relatively cost-effective mechanism to maintain the control of remote frontier areas, which would otherwise be a very expensive endeavor. Indeed, as an institutionalized practice, banishing outcasts to remote regions serve at least two functions for the Chinese state and society: reducing both the burden of dealing with social outcasts in China proper and cost of maintaining and controlling the frontier region.

During the Qing Dynasty, exiled criminals and other social undesirables constituted one of the largest population resettlements in Xinjiang, next only to the military personnel dispatched there for land reclamation and territorial maintenance (Perdue 2005, 348–349). As Perdue states, "By one estimate, about 160,000 exiles went to Xinjiang from 1758 to 1911" (Perdue 2005, 348). Disgraced governmental officials constituted a significant part of the exiled population to Xinjiang. In 1794 alone, "no fewer than 445 former officials were living in exile in Xinjiang" (Seymour and Anderson 1998, 13). These governmental personnel covered a wide spectrum of official titles and profiles from lower rank to very high levels in the administrative hierarchy. It was found, for example, that more than ten percent of the Governors-General under Qing rule were exiled to Xinjiang between 1758 and 1820. Sometimes, when found guilty, a whole group of officials involved in a criminal case could be impeached and exiled collectively. Such a case happened in 1781 when more than fifty officials were banished to Xinjiang from the neighboring province of Gansu over one corruption scandal (Perdue 2005, 349). Governmental officials did not even have to be convicted of crime to find themselves among the rank of the exiled. Issues as petty as misconduct or poor job performance, and "failure to prevent deficit" (Perdue 2005, 349), for example, would be sufficient enough reason for their banishment to Xinjiang.

The practice of exiling convicts to frontier areas had different connotations for the governments on the one hand and for the convicts and their families on the other. For the former, it was the most convenient, cost-effective, and therefore preferred approach to deal with the convicts. For the latter, however, it was the cruelest treatment that they should expect to receive, next only to execution in terms of the severity of the punishment (Seymour and Anderson 1998, 12). To fully understand the practical and symbolic meanings entailed in the practice of exiling convicts to frontier areas in China, we need to review the cultural, geographic, environmental, and demographic characteristics of Xinjiang as well as its relations with China proper.

First, the remoteness of Xinjiang plays a major role in the region being the preferred destination of migration of convicts from inner China. As was mentioned in chapter 1, Xinjiang is a vast territory located far away from China's cultural and economic centers. The distance between Urumqi, which has been the capital city of Xinjiang since the Qing government proclaimed the region one of its provinces in 1884, and Beijing is more than three thousand kilometers (close to nineteen hundred miles). We should be reminded, besides, that within Xinjiang, Urumqi is relatively proximate to inland China—the distance is even more faraway between remote areas in Xinjiang and China proper.

It is, therefore, not difficult to imagine the amount of time it would take and hardship one would have to endure to travel from anywhere in China proper to Xinjiang, or vice versa, particularly during times when long-distance traveling could not be facilitated by anything other than caravans, horses, and things alike. Even when traveling was made much easier by motor vehicles in recent times, it still would take months to travel from the eastern part of China to Xinjiang during the first half of the 20th century (Teichman 1927). The shear remoteness of Xinjiang, in other words, helps explain the Chinese government's motivation to dispose convicts from all over China to Xinjiang. It was sort of an "out of sight, out of mind" mentality being put into practice. To convicts, however, the long distance between Xinjiang and their homeland often meant a life and death journey or permanent separation from their families once they found themselves on the Xinjiang-bound journey.

Second, Xinjiang's environmental and physical conditions are drastically different from those in most of China proper. The atmosphere in Xinjiang is very dry and arid with little rainfall and drastic temperature changes from area to area, season to season, and even between day and night. Furthermore, Xinjiang's landscape is unique in China. In addition to huge mountain ranges, a significant portion of Xinjiang consists of large stretches of Gobi desert, which is not suitable for human inhabitation.[3] Due to all these geographic and ecological conditions, there are major differences in terms of economic activities, the way of living and lifestyles between Xinjiang and eastern parts of China. For example, Xinjiang's agricultural production is completely dependent on irrigation. Access to and control of water resources, consequently, are essential in the sustenance of all populations in the region. The convicts and migrants from east of Xinjiang had to learn and develop skills and capabilities to gain access to water, which often involved competition and maneuvering of relationships with other populations, particularly aboriginal populations. All these difficulties and hardships entail different meanings, again, for the exiled convicts and for the government. For the former, they pose great challenges, dangers, and threats just to survive, but for the latter, these conditions simply help enhance the effectiveness and harshness of the intended punishment of convicts.

Finally, arguably the most important reason for exiling convicts to Xinjiang had to do with the deeply racist ideology and mentality of Chinese mainstream culture, as was discussed in the previous chapter. Demographic compositions in the frontier region of Xinjiang are drastically different from those in China proper. Most of the ethnic populations in Xinjiang are different from the Han Chinese in terms of not only economic pursuit and lifestyle, but also physiological appearance and primordialist and cultural characteristics such as language, religion, ethnicity, kinship, and value systems. For example, many ethnic populations in Xinjiang are Turkic Muslims with their own languages and other cultural features. For millennia, the dominant Chinese culture holds heavily prejudiced, discriminatory, and racist viewpoints toward minority ethnic populations in frontier regions, considering them to be inferior to the Chinese population and culture (e.g., Dreyer 1976; Harrell 1990, 1997 (a); Newby 1988; Perdue 2005, 338). It was commonplace for the Han Chinese to refer to ethnic minority groups with derogative terminologies and expressions at both informal and official settings (Dwyer 2004; Harrell 1990, 1997 (a) and (b); McKhann 1997).

The supremacist mentality and attitude toward ethnic minorities played a major role in the practice of banishing officials to Xinjiang. Based on the Confucian philosophical orientation, that officials show absolute obedience to the higher-up authority constituted one of the major principles that was believed to help maintain social order. Consequently, when governmental officials were convicted of crime, they were viewed, by the royal court as well as their peers, as having violated not only legal codes, but also social regulations, moral standards, and the institutional establishment (Seymour and Anderson 1998). The stigma and humiliation were even more augmented when disgraced officials were banished to the frontier region. Not only did they become social outcasts in the circle of officialdom, they also had to travel thousands of kilometers away from a high culture to what was conceived to be a backward and uncivilized remote region. In addition, they had to endure hardships and destitution and deal with people they considered to be barbarous and of no equal status to the dominant Han people and culture.

While in exile, some of the governmental officials were given official duties that they were expected to perform. However, it was often assumed by Han officials that aboriginal populations were so backward and uncivilized that they were no different from lower level animals and therefore they should not be treated with the type of management mechanisms applicable to the mainstream Chinese culture and society. Exiled officials sometimes would only be expected to do things equivalent to setting up equipment and facilities to control animal-like creatures, sheep, for example, so they would not cause too much damage. As one researcher points out, the expectation was that the local populations should be tamed to the extent that they would not "leap the fences, bite through the bamboo screens, and wander far to trample the young crops" (Dreyer 1976, 14).

PRC'S POLICIES OF MIGRATION TO AND SOCIAL CONTROL IN XINJIANG

Even though the PRC was founded on the framework of equal status of regions and peoples of all ethnic backgrounds, it nonetheless adopted policies that, to an extent, reinforced historical patterns of using frontier regions as dumping areas for social undesirables. The most illustrative of these institutionalized practices is the deportation of prisoners from eastern parts of China to Xinjiang and other remote regions for the purpose of *laogai* (labor and reform).[4] According to one study, there were at least 123 thousand, or as many as 160 thousand, Bingtuan prisoners in Xinjiang during the early 1950s with nearly all of them being deported from the eastern part of China (Seymour 2000, 174). These prisoners were enrolled in dozens of prison (*laogai*) camps or jails (*kanshousuo*) within Bingtuan's correctional system (Seymour and Anderson 1998, 65).

In addition to banishing prisoners to Xinjiang, the PRC government also encouraged a large number of Han migrants from the eastern part of China to Xinjiang. As has been observed by many researchers, officially organized or facilitated migrations to Xinjiang have been routine practices adopted by Chinese governments for both practical and ideological reasons for at least two millennia (Millward 2007, 251–254; Perdue 2005, 333–353; Toops

2004). Migrants were needed for land reclamation and jobs associated with the region's development. More importantly, the increase of the Han population in the region helped with China's control of Xinjiang.

Compared with dynastic rulers of China, the PRC government is far more successful in increasing the Han population through migration to Xinjiang. As was discussed in chapter 1, the first large group of Han settlers in Xinjiang after 1949 consisted mostly of roughly 100 thousand former soldiers of either the Communist or Nationalist armies who were practically ordered to settle in Xinjiang once they were discharged from military duties. Since most of them were young males, the government recruited a large number of Han young females from central and eastern parts of China and sent them to Xinjiang in order to offset the extremely imbalanced sex ratio of Han population in the region (Joniak-Lüthi 2013). Nearly all of the women eventually settled down in Xinjiang by marrying male Han migrants.

Managing Han migrants in Xinjiang has been proven to be a challenging issue. Between 1957 and 1960, more than 800 thousand people made the journey to Xinjiang (Joniak-Lüthi 2013, 164). Many of them were farmers who went to Xinjiang to escape the destitution of their hometowns. But even they were reluctant to settle in rural or minority dominant areas of Xinjiang. Within just nine months in 1957, for example, 20 thousand people poured into the cities of Xinjiang, forming a "blind influx of masses" (Schwarz 1963, 63). The government of Xinjiang had to adopt measures to get these new migrants to settle in the countryside or persuade them to return to their original hometown.

With the economic reform, Xinjiang saw a significant decrease of Han in-migration and a surge of return migration of Han people out of the region. These are reasons that according to census data, there was a noticeable drop of the proportion of Han population in Xinjiang from 40.41 percent in 1982 to 37.58 percent in 1990. Xinjiang-bound migration picked up again starting from the 1990s and took place at a rate comparable with the level of migration to some of the most developed cities in the coastal region at that time (Joniak-Lüthi 2013, 167). However, there were major differences in terms of patterns of migration to Xinjiang prior to and after the reform. The post-reform migration has been mostly in response to economic opportunities in Xinjiang brought about by the reform. Compared with earlier settlers, recent migrants tend to be temporary and seasonal. They move to Xinjiang mostly for economic gains but are not likely to be committed to a long-term settlement in the region. The waves of violence and riots in Xinjiang since the 1990s have only made Xinjiang even less attractive for long-term settlement for the Han population (Joniak-Lüthi 2013).

The many terrorist attacks in Xinjiang throughout the 1990s, referred to as "Islamic terrorism" or "Uyghur terrorism" by both the Chinese government and scholars (China Daily 2003; Vicziany 2003), were subjects of numerous studies (e.g., Hierman 2007; Millward 2004; Vicziary 2003). Researchers offer various explanations for the rise of violence in Xinjiang. Some argue that it is part of a global movement that indicated a severe clash between the Islamic religion and western ideology (Amineh 2007; Li, X. 2002; Li and Niemann 2016). Some suggest that the conflicts resulted mostly from a Pan-Turkic nationalist ideology and the Uyghur people's desire to build an autonomous entity in Xinjiang free of Chinese influences (Hyer 2006, 80–81). Others make a connection between the violence and the declaration of independence by former Soviet republics and the renewed exchange of cultural and religious dialogues and practices across the border (Bovingdon 2004; Mackerras 2001). Still others believe that the Uyghur people's resentment is a reaction to the many changes brought about by the reform, such as the increasing disparities in terms of the distribution of the tremendous economic gains (Heilig 2006), the constant Han migration to Xinjiang, and the environmental damage that Xinjiang has experienced (Bovingdon 2004).

The Chinese government provided its own explanations for the social unrest in Xinjiang during the 1990s, attributing it mostly to the relatively relaxed religious and ethnic policies implemented during the previous decade. Based on this sentiment, drastic changes were made to adopt a much more rigorous approach in ethnic relations starting from the mid-1990s (Bovingdon 2004; Millward 2004). At the same time, the assistance program became institutionalized as a mechanism to resolve the problem of racial tension in Xinjiang. As was discussed in chapter 2, at the Polit Bureau Standing Committee of the CCP in 1996, the then president of China, Mr. Jiang Zemin, officially declared the institutionalization of the assistance program with cadre assistance as the major, if not the only, component in Xinjiang.[5]

The assistance program was expanded in 2005 to include economic, technological, and cultural assistance, but cadre assistance was still considered the most important element of the program. Jiang's successor, Hu Jintao, was quoted as stating, when commenting on the revised assistance program in 2005, that cadre assistance should be treated as the "dragon's head" (龙头) in the assistance program to Xinjiang (Yang 2008), suggesting the crucial role cadre assistance was expected to play in the assistance program.

After the September 11, 2001 incidence, the vigilance in ethnic minority areas, particularly areas of Muslim populations, became more stringent in China. The subsequent campaigns by Western countries to fight against terrorism at the global level provided the Chinese government with even more impetus to engage in extremely tense operations to control Muslim populations. The strike-hard campaigns to bring about social stability in Xinjiang, however, were proven to be not very effective. The Chinese government, as well as the whole country, were shocked by the worst violence and terrorist incidence in decades that took place in Urumqi on July 5, 2009.

In the search for solutions during the aftermath of the violence, attention was once again turned to the assistance program by the government. Following resolutions made at the two conferences on Xinjiang in 2010,[6] a drastically overhauled version of the assistance program was presented that involved the 19 provincial-level administrative units and municipalities as assistance providers and the whole region of Xinjiang as assistance recipient. Still the dominant part of the program, the cadre assistance has nonetheless experienced noticeable changes, especially from the early years of campaigns, to dispatch cadre and *rencai* (qualified personnel) migrants to Xinjiang.

CADRE AND *RENCAI* MIGRATION TO XINJIANG

Throughout the PRC era, a major challenge in encouraging Xinjiang-bound Han migration has been to entice skilled, educated, and professional individuals. Referred to as *rencai*, these migrants include engineers, nurses, statisticians, health care personnel, teachers, technicians, and other professionals. During the early years of the PRC, these *rencai* migrants were recruited through various means including propaganda of a good life in Xinjiang, ideological indoctrination of patriotism, and advertising of policies of cost-of-living wage subsidies (Joniak-Lüthi 2013; Li, R. 1989; Schwarz 1963, 66–67). These measures were successful to a certain degree. During mid-1950s (1954–1955), at least six thousand, or close to ten thousand, professionals and skilled personnel were sent to Xinjiang by the central government and by various provinces or cities in eastern China (Schwarz 1963, 63–64 and 68–69).

In spite of the government's great efforts, however, the proportion of *rencai* in the total pool of Xinjiang-bound migrants kept dwindling from close to 15 percent in the 1950s to less than 4 percent during the 1970s. The reduction was caused by two mutually reinforcing factors. One was the high rate of return migration by *rencai* personnel. The second factor was that the number of *rencai* migrants moving to Xinjiang decreased rapidly over the decades. The relatively large flow of *rencai* migration during the previous years was largely due to the government's control of population mobility and the registration system. As Joniak-Lüthi (2013) points out, the state was able to assign thousands of college graduates to Xinjiang annually during the early 1980s. Many of them, however, went to Xinjiang with a great degree of reluctance and it was not surprising they would choose to join the flow of return migration whenever there was an opportunity. Furthermore, it became much more difficult to recruit *rencai* migrants to Xinjiang and other frontier areas once the state-controlled planned system was dismantled and the government could no longer control the population mobility after the 1980s.

In addition to skilled professionals, another type of highly sought-after *rencai* migrants to Xinjiang are cadre members who were recruited to achieve the various political and ideological missions of the CCP in Xinjiang. Specifically, they were needed to help with the implementation of governmental plans, spreading the Party ideology, maintaining social stability and the performance of various administrative and professional duties. In a word, cadres played roles that were essential to ensuing CCP's control of Xinjiang. During the beginning years of the PRC, cadre migrants were mostly drawn from veterans because they tended to be politically loyal and committed to CCP's ideology (Schwarz 1963).

Cadre members were needed in not only cities and Han-dominant communities, such as *Bingtuan*, but more importantly in areas predominantly inhabited by minority populations where there was a high level of resentment and hostility against Han control. A large number of Han cadre members had to be recruited within a short period of time during the early PRC years. Several measures were adopted to deal with the problem of cadre shortage at that time. One was to send delegates to the eastern part of the country to recruit cadre personnel (Schwarz 1963). The other measure was to give priority to the quantity rather than quality of recruited cadre. Still another measure was to select candidates from ethnic minority populations who were viewed as being transformable into Party members or political activists (McMillen 1979, 85–86). In all these situations, intense training and constant evaluation of the newly recruited cadres were conducted to ensure that they perform duties as expected.

One of the greatest challenges brought about by the reform is the difficulty for the government to generate *rencai* or cadre migration to Xinjiang. The large volume of return migration from Xinjiang since the reform, as was discussed above, has been disproportionately represented by *rencai* and cadre members. This resulted in the serious problem of "brain drain" in Xinjiang,[7] which reflects the dilemma of post-reform migration policies in China. On the one hand, the government wishes to be able to control the population mobility and organize Xinjiang-bound migrations whenever necessary. On the other hand, however, market forces tend to dictate the flow of the labor force, including *rencai* migration (Li, Q. 2017). These contradictions and the dilemma are most readily revealed in policies and changes in the 2010 version of cadre assistance programs in Xinjiang.

CADRE ASSISTANCE PROGRAM IN XINJIANG SINCE 2010

Changes in the 2010 cadre assistance program are made at both the central government level, as well as the provincial and individual city levels that provide cadre assistance. The first major change was that, compared with previous times, a significantly larger number of cadre members were sent to Xinjiang from participating provinces and municipalities in the assistance program, as well as from state-owned companies and various departments and organizations directly under the central government. According to an official news report in *Xinjiang Daily* published in September 2014, a total of roughly 7,000 cadre individuals were sent to Xinjiang during the first seventeen years of the assistance program (1997–2013). In comparison, during the first nine months of 2014 alone, more than 4,000 Xinjiang-bound cadre members made the journey (CPC News 2014). Another official source, the 2015 Xinjiang Yearbook, quotes the total number of *rencai* that had been sent to Xinjiang in 2014 to be as many as 9,282 (*Xinjiang Yearbook* 2015, 130).

In addition to the increased volume of participation, there is also a shift of the way "cadre assistance" was conceptualized. There is a tremendous overlapping between the categories of cadre and *rencai* in China's occupational structure. Many cadre members with administrative duties are at the same time professionals and skilled personnel, and vice versa, hence they are often generally referred to as "*ganbu rencai*," meaning cadre professionals or cadre *rencai*. For example, it is mentioned that in 2011, a total of 267 *ganbu rencai* were sent from Hubei to its matching partner of Bortala Mongol Autonomous Prefecture in Xinjiang. Among them, as was further pointed out, there were 49 cadres, 113 teachers, 65 doctors, and 40 other technical and professional personnel (*Xinjiang Yearbook* 2012, 159). The number of technical and professional personnel in various fields far outnumbered that of cadre. This phenomenon was also commented on by Mr. Zhang Chunxian, the Party secretary of Xinjiang from 2010 to 2016, who stated: The cadre assistance to Xinjiang experienced many changes, from a single category of personnel to a diverse group of people with a wide variety of professions and occupations (CPC News 2014). These diverse "cadre *rencai*" represent a wide range of professional fields including medical professionals, teachers, and those with expertise in agricultural production, irrigation systems, animal husbandry, tourism, construction, and engineering (Xinjiang Yearbooks).

Furthermore, there are also changes in the approach to recruit cadre professionals. In addition to the standard recruitment strategy, alternative methods were used for the recruitment. According to official reports, there is a targeted plan for the numbers and types of cadre assistance each year in the whole assistance program as well as in each of the 19 participating provinces or municipalities. For example, the Beijing government was said to be the first participating unit in 2010 to submit proposals to relevant agencies for approval concerning its plan for cadre assistance to Xinjiang. In addition, many provinces and municipalities have also sent, and are encouraged to send, people who are not part of the plan through a mechanism that is referred to as "outside plan (*jihuawai*)" *rencai*. What this means is that extra steps were expected to be taken by participating administrative units or organizations to enhance cadre assistance. A case in point is volunteers who are solicited to join the course of *rencai* assistance. For instance, Shenzhen reported that of the 187 cadre and *rencai* assistance personnel that the city sent to Kashgar in 2011, about one-third (63) were volunteers (Xinjiang Yearbook 2012, 160).

The pursuit of the unconventional methods to channel talents to underdeveloped regions is attempted by both the deliverers and recipients of the assistance program. The various alternative approaches to attract participants to join the personnel assistance described above are part of what is referred to as "flexible personnel assistance (*rouxing rencai yuanjiang*)," which has become an increasingly routine method adopted by relatively less-developed regions in China to attract talents. When people with credentials or expertise are recruited following the approach of flexible personnel assistance, they do not have to follow conventional procedures, such as changing their registration or residential status or meeting other bureaucratic requirements, to be considered part of the assistance team. All they need to do is to offer "guidance, instructions, demonstrations and lectures" to the recipient area (Xinhuanet 2012). According to one report, the approach of flexible personnel assistance has been proven effective in generating positive results to help facilitate the development of the assistance recipient area.[8]

There is a concerted effort by both the central government and the 19 administrative assistance deliverers to regulate, systematize, and ultimately entice cadre and other personnel assistance to Xinjiang. The Bureau of Public Health and Bureau of Education of China, for example, both published documents with specific information and instructions concerning the selection procedure, eligibility, and qualification requirements of personnel to participate in assistance programs to Tibet and Xinjiang. These documents provide detailed guidelines concerning how to implement the cadre assistance, the desired number of cadre and professional members to be recruited, the process of the recruitment, the duration of terms of service, the expected professional responsibilities and the benefit packages for the participation, and so on (Zinan 2010). In addition to the kind of ideological outlook consistent with the Party's guidelines, as was stated by Mr. Jiang Zemin discussed earlier, the following four points have been frequently made regarding these policies:

First, educational background and credentials, as well as demographic characteristics, are established criteria for the selection of participants. For example, some personnel recruiters require that the people who are dispatched must have at least an associate (*dazhuan*) degree. An age requirement (not older than 55 for cadres and 45 for professional personnel) is specified in some documents.

Second, a wide range of financial compensations as rewards for participation in the program are listed in nearly all documents. They include pay increases, bonuses, stipends, insurance coverages, travel and living expense compensations for both the participants themselves as well as their family members, and financial benefit to their families such as health care, day care, and educational cost. In addition, in order for the participants to serve their duties in Xinjiang worry-free, their families enjoy welfare benefits that are not otherwise available. Spouses of dispatched personnel are not to be laid off, for instance, even in the event that being laid off is a likely occurrence at the place of their employment.

The document concerning personnel assistance to Xinjiang by the city of Shaoxing in Zhejiang Province produced in 2010 is an illustrative example. According to the document, the following rewards and benefits would be awarded to participants in the assistance program to Xinjiang: (1) Participants receive a one-step pay increase and their salary would be issued by their work unit in their original area of assistance delivery. (2) They receive an additional monthly stipend of 2,000 yuan while in Xinjiang. (3) They receive a 10,000 yuan compensation for clothes for the preparation for the trip and a life expense compensation of 8,000 yuan for one year stay and 15,000 yuan for three year stay in Xinjiang. (4) Their spouses are allowed to reside in the assistance destination if they would like to, should not be laid off during the assistance stay, and should be reassigned employment in the event of their work unit declaring bankruptcy. (5) Their spouses enjoy a paid trip (by the assistance personnel's original unit) of one month if the assistance is for one year, three months if the assistance is for three years. (6) The participants' work units in the assistance delivery location have the responsibility of taking care of the financial cost of day care, education as well as an annual health check that their children are entitled to (Xinjiang Wenxue Net 2010).

The third noticeable point in the policies is the advantageous prospect of job and career advancement for participants in the assistance program. Most individuals who are sent to Xinjiang are expected to serve administrative or professional duties that correspond to their occupational and professional responsibilities at their original work site location (Yaxin 2010). Not only does participation in the assistance program have no negative impact on their career patterns and development, but it is viewed very positively in the evaluation of the participants' job performance and possible career advancement. Participants in assistance programs are often allowed to waive major requirements for promotion or employment upgrade, for example, foreign language and other job-related proficiency tests (Wenzhou Dangjian 2016). If the assistance personnel were teachers, the participation in the assistance program could be considered the tenure of teaching at school systems in less-developed and rural areas, which, by law, would give them an advantage to receive job-related compensation and promotion (Editing Group of Compulsory Education 2006, 356–357).

Indeed, the experience of participating in the Xinjiang assistance program seems to be a secure stepping-stone to job promotions and professional upward mobility (Xiangya 2011). For instance, one news report mentions three individuals from a city in Zhejiang Province who had been sent to Xinjiang to participate in the assistance program during the 1990s. When the report was written in 2010, all of them had experienced significant promotions in the hierarchical occupational structure (Yaxin 2010). Another report comments that the candidate for the position of mayor of Zhenjiang City, Jiangsu Province, Mr. Zhang Yefei (张叶飞), had served as the party secretary of Huocheng County in Yili of Xinjiang during his participation in the assistance program to Xinjiang from 2008 to 2011 (SINA 2016). This reference was made with a positive tone in favor of Mr. Zhang's candidacy as the potential mayor.

The pattern of evaluation of cadres' participation in the Xinjiang assistance program is consistent with China's efforts to reform the system of overall job evaluations for cadre. Increasingly, job and career evaluations of cadre members in China are based on concrete, measurable, and specific activities and performances that could be clearly operationalized using the quantitative measure and a point system, as is indicated by Whiting (2004). Not only is the participation itself, but specific details such as the length and location of services, tasks performed and other relevant variables associated with the assistance program participation are all taken into consideration and given weight in the evaluations. In addition, since the assistance program to Xinjiang is a national campaign initiated by the Beijing authority, bureaucratic organizations of various levels are held accountable for their compliance with the policies. As is generally the case in China, the extent to which top-down policies are carried out and implemented would have a significant impact on evaluations of and possible upward mobility for governmental officials at various levels (Holbig 2004; Shih 2004; Whiting 2004). In other words, it is at least partly for the sake of career advancement of officials themselves that they see to it that programs concerning cadre assistance are well-planned, carefully organized, and thoroughly implemented.

Finally, perhaps the most intriguing aspect of the 2010 version of the cadre assistance program is that it specifically states that the tenure for participation in the program is three years for cadre members and a year and half for professional and technical personnel. This limited tenure duration requirement and the aggressive and various efforts to recruit cadre and talents from the 19 provinces and municipalities for service in the assistance program are indicative of the difficulties in generating participation in the program. As was discussed earlier, the PRC is much more successful compared with preceding rulers of China for thousands of years to lure Han settlements to Xinjiang. Much of this outcome was attributable to PRC's strictly planned and authoritarian political, social, and economic arrangements prior to the reform, which enabled the government to organize both voluntary and involuntary Xinjiang-bound migrations. Many migrants ultimately settled in the region, including cadres, professional and technical personnel, farmers, soldiers, and criminals and social undesirables.

The situation is very different, however, during the 21st century when China has been pursuing a hybrid development model of "socialism with Chinese characteristics." Thanks to its authoritarian state power, China has been able to utilize organizational and institutional resources to produce attractive benefit packages and make flexible arrangements to entice cadre and professional personnel to participate in the program. At the same time, however, it is not nearly as easy as in previous years to mobilize elite members from the eastern part of China to Xinjiang when it no longer has the ability to exercise absolute control over the lives of individuals. As a result, the relatively short-term tenure required of participation in the assistance program is perhaps a measure of compromise. Even with the handsome benefit package and the limited duration of required tenure, there still seems to be a great degree of reluctance and unwillingness for participation in the program. One cadre member from southern China who was in the assistance program in northern Xinjiang commented in summer 2016:

> When I was growing up, one of my neighbors had a relative in Xinjiang. It would take him four days and nights by train to get home from Xinjiang. Besides, he also had to take a long bus ride before boarding on a train in Xinjiang. To me at that time, Xinjiang was so remote and so far that I never imagined that I would go there.
>
> When asked whether he was enthusiastic to be part of the assistance team, he replied,
>
> Well, not really. But when I was approached (by the authority) about this matter, I really did not have a good enough reason to say no. My only child is grown and has left home and I am in good health. So I realized that it was sort of my turn to do this.[9]

A medical doctor from a municipality in the coastal area who was in the assistance program in southern Xinjiang made the following remark during an interview in summer 2014:

> It is not really a pleasant experience. Being outsiders, we are very concerned about our safety here since there have been so many violent incidences. But it is supposed to be only a temporary stay for us, and I try to look at the positive side. This experience will help me with my career advancement. Besides, my

> family have joined me in Xinjiang while I am here and we have traveled in both southern and northern Xinjiang. We would not have had such opportunities to see so much of Xinjiang if it were not for me to participate in the assistance program.[10]

To a certain extent, the disinclination and lack of enthusiasm in participating in the program are attributable to geographic, environmental, and cultural differences between Xinjiang and the rest of China, as was discussed earlier in this chapter. Even though the improvement of transportation and communication facilities has helped ease the complication and difficulties brought about by the remoteness and distance of the region, as far as cadre and *rencai* are concerned, who are among elite members of the society, the huge gap between the western region and the rest of China in terms of economic and social development since the reform has just added to the degree of unattractiveness of Xinjiang, as well as the whole western region. Researchers have frequently observed deep-rooted prejudicial attitudes by mainstream Chinese society, including even educated young Han people in Xinjiang, including the city of Urumqi, against the western region and ethnic minority populations (Caprioni 2012; Yee 2005). Based on her research on the attitude of young Han people in Urumqi concerning Xinjiang and the Uyghur population, Caprioni points out: The feeling of Xinjiang's marginal status in China "not only blunts the Communist government's achievements of developing the western frontier region, but also indicates that popular misconceptions of Xinjiang as remote and underdeveloped, which date back to the previous generations, are still present in everyday culture and find new life in young Hans today" (Caprioni 2012, 131).

Arguably the most irksome issue among the obstacles in the government's attempt to mobilize cadre and *rencai* assistance to Xinjiang is the relentless and escalating violence in the region, which is at least part of the very reason for the drastic intensification of the assistance program. The situation is particularly serious in southern Xinjiang. The CCP Xinjiang Committee held two meetings in recent years to address this issue: the seventh session of the committee's eighth conference in June 2014 and the southern Xinjiang work conference (新疆维吾尔自治区党委南疆工作会议) held in Kashgar in November 2015. The latter was said to be the very first meeting by the provincial government to focus specifically on cadre-related issues in southern Xinjiang. The following points were made at both meetings: (1) Xinjiang's priority should be devoted to efforts of anti-splittism and anti-terrorism and on maintaining stability in the region; and (2) Economic development and infrastructure construction would continue to receive primary attention so that Xinjiang was to become a moderately prosperous (*xiaokang*) region with no more poverty counties by 2020.

In order to achieve these goals, states the provincial party chief Zhang Chunxian, it is essential to have a sufficient presence of *rencai* and cadre members in Xinjiang, particularly southern Xinjiang. According to Zhang, southern Xinjiang has had a long history of having difficulty attracting and maintaining (Han) cadre members. To solve this problem, he continues, an unusual measure (*chaochanggui jucue*) would be implemented that utilizes both administrative measures and market mechanism to recruit cadre to Xinjiang. Specifically, the following elements would be implemented: (1) enriching and enhancing the benefit package and incentives for cadre and *rencai* who work in southern Xinjiang, (2) developing opportunities for them to receive training and education, and (3) establishing a system whereby cadre members in various part of Xinjiang rotate their work sites. Zhang also warned at the meetings that other regions and districts in Xinjiang should not be jealous or unhappy about the preferential policies and special treatment that southern Xinjiang receives. Instead, they should try to be considerate of the difficult situation in Xinjiang and actively support the special arrangement that the government had made for southern Xinjiang (CPCNews 2015; Tianshan Net 2015; Xinjiang Tianshan 2014).

SUMMARY

Cadre members and other professionals who are sent to Xinjiang play instrumental roles in spreading the CCP ideology and enhancing the legitimacy of the CCP control of Xinjiang. Consequently, cadre assistance to Xinjiang is viewed to be essential in maintaining Xinjiang's stability under the CCP rule. However, for centuries, Xinjiang has been associated with a very negative sentiment within the Han Chinese society. In addition to geographic and climatic characteristics, prejudice based on cultural differences between Xinjiang and the Han Chinese society is also responsible for the unfavorable image of Xinjiang. Because of all these reasons, Han Chinese, especially elite members such as the cadre, generally feel reluctant to move to Xinjiang.

The situation has been exacerbated by the fact that Xinjiang has been routinely used as a "dumping ground" for social undesirables from the eastern part of China and that there has been escalating racial violence in Xinjiang in recent years. All these circumstances have made it difficult for the Chinese government to expand the cadre assistance program in Xinjiang despite special measures and policies to entice professionals and cadres to participate in the program. Generous assistance and support for rapid economic development in the region makes up a significant component of such measures and policies, as will be discussed in the next chapter.

NOTES

1. There is a high degree of membership overlapping between political party (the CCP) members and those who occupy civil services occupations (the state) with the former being recognized as being much more prestigious and powerful compared with the latter. This is the reason the cadre management system in China is referred to as *nomenklatura* by researchers. Efforts to reform the system at the beginning of the reform to separate the Party and the state failed after the 1989 student movement in China. This issue, as well as the overall political reform, have not been brought back to the agenda of China's reforms since then (Lam and Chan 1996; Naughton and Yang 2004, 13).

2. The most important components of the indoctrination include messages about the significance of stability in the region and Xinjiang being an integral part of China.

3. The Taklamakan desert in southern Xinjiang has been labeled "the worst desert on earth" (Blackmore 1995).

4. A law was passed in China in 1954 titled "Regulations on Reform through Labor" which officially made the concept of "reform through labor" (*laodong gaizao*, or, in short form, *laogai*) the cornerstone of China's judicial system. To facilitate this law, a large number of labor camps were set up in many parts of the country, particularly in the northwestern region, including Xinjiang, Gansu, and Qinghai, for the purpose of reforming prisoners and other offenders. Frontier provinces and regions were never involved in the decision-making process of having prisoners deported to their territories, but they demonstrated very little resistance under the centrally planned system of social, political, and economic arrangements of the PRC (Seymour and Anderson 1998).

5. See chapter 2 for the two meetings on Xinjiang.

6. Please see chapter 2 for discussion on the conferences.

7. This problem is not limited to Xinjiang only. The idiomatic expression of "peacock flying to the southeast" is used to refer to the migration pattern since the reform of a large number of *rencai* and professionals moving to the coastal southeastern China from other parts of the country for higher pay and more abundant resources.

8. It was reported that as a result of the involvement of 80 or so academicians recruited with the approach of flexible personal assistance, academics in Ningxia Hui Autonomous Region had received more research funding and produced more research publications (Xinhuanet 2012).

9. Interview conducted by the author in northern Xinjiang in summer 2016.

10. Interview conducted by the author in southern Xinjiang in summer 2014.

Chapter 5

Economic Development and Assistance Program in Xinjiang

The economic assistance to Xinjiang has been carefully crafted and staged by the PRC government, similar to the overall development of the region (Becquelin 2004). But the Chinese government's ability to control and shape Xinjiang's economy has always been constrained by numerous factors that are not within the government's immediate control. One factor is the long history of interactions between rulers of China and the Central Asian region as well as those among the many empires and tribes in the region. It was through thousands of years of difficult attempts and pains-taking efforts that China finally gained control over Xinjiang. The high level of economic spending and financial cost associated with maintaining control over the remote and underdeveloped region has been a serious consideration for rulers of China. As will be discussed below, the current economic assistance programs are, to a great extent, an extension and modification of strategies instigated by China's rulers of various dynastic periods to maintain their relationship with Xinjiang.

Another factor that China has little control over is the impact of countries and territories across the border from Xinjiang and other powerful forces in the global arena that try to manipulate the strategically important area where Xinjiang is located. Examples of such forces and their influences include the impact of Buddhism during the Jin Dynasty (265–420) (Millward 2007, 27–28) and the 'Great Games" participated by Great Britain and Russia/USSR at the end of the 19th century and the beginning of the 20th century. The dynamic and complicated relations among all these forces have significantly shaped and changed the economic conditions of Xinjiang.

Finally, the geographic, demographic, environmental, and cultural features of Xinjiang have also played important roles in determining Xinjiang's economy and the effectiveness of the economic "assistance" orchestrated by the PRC government. For example, the heavy emphasis on economic projects such as the development of technological and industrial parks since 2010 constitutes a significant part in the recent assistance program in Xinjiang. But, as the discussion below will illustrate, there is much uncertainty concerning the long-term impact of this approach due to the unique geographic, demographic and cultural features of the region.

ASSISTANCE TO XINJIANG'S ECONOMY BY DYNASTIC RULERS OF CHINA

The earliest significant penetration of Xinjiang by the Chinese state was under the Han Dynasty (206 BCE–AD 220) when the Chinese empire dispatched sizable military forces to the region. Apart from combating the mighty Xiongnu nomadic group, the Han soldiers engaged in the institutionalization of military farms named "*tuntian.*" *Tuntian* was a system of colonization whereby the Han colonizers relied on land reclamation for cultivation and economic self-sustenance. By encouraging the practice of *tuntian*, subsequent rulers of China strategized that they would not have to provide financial subsidies to Han migrants in the region and at the same time these outsiders would not have to pose too many financial burdens on local populations either, hence making their insertion and penetration relatively smooth and effective (Millward 2007, 21–22). The *tuntian* system, in other words, could be viewed as the earliest attempts by the Chinese state to "assist" not only its campaigns to control the frontier region but also the economy of Xinjiang (Di Cosmo 2009). It is of little surprise that *tuntian* has since been practiced, albeit intermittently, by rulers of China and continued well into the 21st century.

In addition to the *tuntian* system, the Han Dynasty's penetration of Xinjiang left another legacy that has had a significant and long-lasting impact on Xinjiang's economy. Chinese migrants to the region brought with them desirable goods and items, such as silk and tea, with which they participated in the active trade endeavors between China and the West. These trade and commercial exchanges took place along the Silk Road, the most famous trade route in the world for centuries to come. The numerous hub communities along the Silk Road, with many of them located in current Xinjiang, have remained economic, political and cultural centers. The Tang Dynasty of China (618–907) saw probably the most prosperous and active economic and commercial development along the Silk Road.

In spite of China's ambitions to keep firm control of the *xiyu* (western) region, the Chinese presence there was frequently challenged by not only local states of Turkic and other ethnic groups, but also the expanding Mongol empire and Tibetan invaders, among other militant forces. This was one of the reasons that the Chinese influence, or even presence, in Xinjiang was often indirect and intermittent during two millennia. As a matter of fact, for hundreds of years between the Tang Dynasty and the Qing Dynasty (1644–1911), China only ruled the region indirectly with minimum presence in Xinjiang (Millward 2007, 37–39; Sheng 1998). During this long period of time, it was mostly the Soghdians (Iranian) merchants who dominated the commercial activities along the Silk Road (Hansen 1998; Millward 2007; Sheng 1998).

This situation started to change during the Qing Dynasty, which very aggressively expanded China's territory by claiming, for example, large stretches of lands of Central Asia including current Xinjiang. These expeditions, nevertheless, were not without controversies and objections within the Qing court. The huge financial and economic burden associated with the territorial conquest and occupation of the *xiyu* region was a major consideration for the opposition by some in the court.[1] Nonetheless, it seemed emperors of the Qing rule were all steadfastly determined to continue the penetration of and expansion into what would later be known as Xinjiang. Emperor Kangxi, for example, was quoted as having stated that he would not mind spending several times more than what was assumed to be the budget needed for the campaigns to conquer and maintain the frontier territories in Central Asia (Perdue 2005, 230–232).

At the same time, the Qing Court was fully aware that it would be nearly impossible to control the frontier regions unless there was a sizable population settlement from the interior regions of China. Hence, the Qing government made strategic plans to send large waves of migrants, including soldiers, prisoners, farmers, skilled personnel and others, to Xinjiang.[2] For example, a troop of 50,000 soldiers, including the Han, Manchu and Mongol, were stationed in Xinjiang by the mid-19th century (Millward 2007, 97–99). Meanwhile, the Emperor and the Court realized that it would be too costly an endeavor to supply financial resources from the capital of China to Xinjiang to fund salaries of soldiers, the officers and administrators and other maintenance costs. It was therefore decided that the key to the success of controlling Xinjiang was, again, the adequate development of the local economy so that the army and other migrants could be self-sufficient. As Emperor Kangxi stated, with a supremacist tone, that communities settled by migrants from the interior "not only save on transport costs, and allow one to exhaust the earth's resources, but they will also make the enemy barbarians disperse to poor areas, while our generals enjoy a peaceful sleep on their pillows and mats" (Perdue 2005, 328).

Historically, Xinjiang's economy was mostly based on agricultural and animal husbandry productions. Herders and farmers had to work collaboratively in order to ensure the sustenance of their respective populations in very harsh natural conditions (Millward 2007, 38). For example, pastoralists relied on farmers for daily necessities such as grains and other food items and settled farmers depended on nomadic herdsmen for desired goods and products, especially those items that were not available locally but could be obtained through long-distance trade and commercial exchanges (Di Cosmo 2009, 1994).

Qing government made Xinjiang an official province of China in 1884 and subsequently engaged in a series of campaigns to stimulate traditional agricultural and animal husbandry productions, as well as other economic activities. The campaigns focused on the commercialization of agriculture, development of handicraft industries and encouragement of trade and commercial activities. Permanent settlement in the region facilitated by the *tuntian* system was emphasized with stimulus measures such as "free allotments of land, seeds, and silver tael earmarked for buying equipment and establishing homes" (Wiemer 2004, 165).

Economic assistance was clearly a significant component of the economic stimulus policies implemented by the Qing government in Xinjiang. These policies were aimed at helping newly arriving migrants to establish themselves in the remote territory. In addition, the Qing government also recruited skilled personnel from other provinces of China to help Xinjiang's technology and alternative methods of conducting agricultural and other economic activities such as cotton and silk weaving (Wiemer 2004, 165).

ASSISTANCE TO XINJIANG'S ECONOMY BY FOREIGN POWERS

Xinjiang's economy was influenced by not only China, but states and powers across the border as well and the foreign powers would often times produce much more of a significant impact upon the local economy as compared with China. Both Tsarist Russia and the Soviet Union had a huge interest in Xinjiang, particularly northern Xinjiang, even though the Soviet Union renounced some of the claims to China's territories that had been made by the Russian Tsars (Fedyshyn 1957). In addition, as the pathway to India, southern Xinjiang became a stronghold of Great Britain at the turn of the 20th century. Not surprisingly, both superpowers emphasized and provided support and assistance to export-oriented economic productions, such as silk and cotton weaving and carpet production, in their respectively controlled territories of northern and southern Xinjiang (Wiemer 2004, 165–166). In addition, trade and commercial exchanges were also heavily manipulated by foreign powers to benefit their own interest. One study published during the 1930s, for example, showed that "nine-tenths of the commerce of Chinese Turkestan is with the USSR" at the time (Vakar 1935, 121). Even during the early years of the PRC, there were still far more trade exchanges between Xinjiang and the Soviet Union than that between Xinjiang and the rest of China.

Xinjiang exported to the Soviet Union agricultural and animal husbandry products and minerals and imported products and material goods for manufacturing and heavy industrial productions, particularly those for the extraction of natural resources (Fedyshyn 1957, 138). Xinjiang is abundant with natural resources such as oil, natural gas, coal, minerals, and rare metals. Despite its reluctance to make long-term investment in Xinjiang during most of its reign (Perdue 2005, 343), the Qing government started to tap into the extraction of Xinjiang's resources toward the end of its rule by recruiting Russian personnel and technology for oil-extraction refinery (Wiemer 2004, 164–165). Oil-drilling efforts and processes in Xinjiang facilitated by the Soviet experts, however, experienced huge obstacles during the first half of the 20th century due to political and social instability in China at that time. In addition, interference in and manipulation of the local economy as well as political maneuvers by the Soviet Union generated suspicions and even resentment from local politicians and populations, which also contributed to the difficulties and complications of developing Xinjiang's industries (McMillen 1979, 7). Indeed, Moscow's ulterior motive to provide assistance to Xinjiang's economy became obviously clear when the USSR proposed a treaty of "friendship, alliance and mutual assistance" between Xinjiang and the Soviet upon the founding of the PRC. By offering financial, technical, material, and personnel assistance to Xinjiang, according to the treaty, the Soviet Union expected Xinjiang to turn over "one-half of Sinkiang's oil and non-ferrous and rare metals" (Fedyshyn 1957, 128).

Despite the self-serving intention of the Soviet Union, its assistance to Xinjiang during the early years of the PRC was well documented by scholars even though China often seemed reluctant to report aid from the USSR (Fedyshyn 1957, 130, 133 and 137–139; McMillen 1979, 163–165). In addition to industrial development, such as construction of plants and facilities for extraction and processing of natural resources, and supply of technology and equipment (McMillen 1979, 164), the Soviet Union also focused on the improvement of transportation infrastructure, such as building roads and airports. It was with Soviet aid and help that some of the very first major roads were built in the vast area of Xinjiang (Field 1961, 315). Indeed, as other researchers have also pointed out, the assistance from the Soviet Union during the early years of the PRC played a major role in the recovery of Xinjiang's economy from decades of war and turmoil. With the China-Soviet relationship going sour at the end of the 1950s and the series of political campaigns that rampaged China during the 1960s and 1970s, however, Xinjiang's economy faltered and suffered periods of severe setbacks (Wiemer 2004), which exacerbated the extent to which the region's economy had to depend on aid from the central government of China.

PRC'S ECONOMIC ASSISTANCE TO XINJIANG

PRC's economic policies concerning Xinjiang resemble those of the Qing Dynasty in the sense that policies on economic development focused on national security and the financial self-sufficiency of the local region (Dreyer 2000, 140; McMillen 1981; Perdue 2005, 335–337; Seymour 2000). Security concerns in Xinjiang derived from two sources. One is interference and potential invasion from across the border and the other is interethnic violence within the region. Similar to the Qing government, the PRC has dealt with security concerns with an influx of Han settlement, including military settlement, in the region. As a result, Xinjiang's total population grew rapidly from less than 5 million in the early 1950s to 20 million by the end of the 20th century. The proportion of Han population escalated from 6 percent to close to 41 percent (Toops 2004), as was discussed in chapter 1.

In the early years of the PRC, all migrants to Xinjiang, including the military, semi-military, and civilians, were expected to be economically self-sufficient because of, again, the simple reason that the central government would not have to bear the burden of providing financial support to them. It was a practical measure in the facilitation of the rapid Han resettlement in Xinjiang. The efforts to achieve self-sufficiency started with large-scale land reclamation and other projects for food and agricultural production. As a result, the area of cultivated land in Xinjiang more than doubled since the PRC era, from 1,543 hectares in 1952 to 3,417 hectares in 2000 (Wiemer 2004, 169).

A significant amount of land reclamation and associated projects, such as construction of irrigation systems, were undertaken by *Bingtuan*. Meanwhile, industrial development has received an increasingly tremendous amount of attention. Within just a few years after the founding of the PRC, *Bingtuan* and the rest of Xinjiang managed to build a strong industrial base with a large number of factories and industrial plants ranging from those for the processing of agricultural and animal husbandry products to those for oil-drilling and processing facilities (Fedyshyn 1957; Li, Y. 2010; McMillen 1979, 163–179). Construction and improvement of transportation systems, including railroad, highway and airport, were also placed at the top of the agenda for economic production, as one author comments, "During the first Five Year Plan a third of all new railway construction in China was laid down in Sinkiang" (Field 1961, 315). In 1958 alone, 3,500 miles of roads were built in Xinjiang (Field 1961, 316). These roads not only connect northern and southern Xinjiang and Xinjiang with the rest of China, but they also extend westward to the Soviet

Union and, via Tibet, India and Pakistan (Field 1961, 317). Needless to say, the improved transportation systems have greatly enhanced the economic performance of the region.

To a great extent, the impressive industrial and infrastructure development in Xinjiang during the early years of the PRC was possible because of the dedication and devotion of citizens in and migrants to Xinjiang. Enduring a great deal of self-sacrifice in terms of work compensation, living conditions, and even food, they overcame extreme physical and material hardships and difficulties in their efforts to build the economy of the region (Li, Y. 2010; McMillen 1979, 165).

A more important reason that helped sustain the rapid development of Xinjiang's economy was financial subsidy and assistance provided by the central government. The realization of self-sufficiency of Xinjiang's economy, as it turned out, proved to be much more difficult than the government had anticipated. Indeed, Xinjiang required such huge volumes of financial and material support and assistance that, as one author points out, "the provincial regime was almost wholly dependent on central economic subsidies" (McMillen 1981, 73). This author also shows that between 1949 and 1958, more than 63 percent of capital investment for economic, cultural and educational development in Xinjiang was provided by the central government with the local revenue contributing only about five percent of the total investment in Xinjiang (McMillen 1979, 164–165).

The central government's assistance and subsidies to Xinjiang were especially substantial during politically unstable times such as the Great Leap Forward movement at the end of the 1950s and the early 1960s and the decade of the Cultural Revolution (1966–1976) when even food had to be transported from other parts of China (Dreyer 2000, 140). These observations are confirmed by data in Column 3 of Table 5.1. In fact, the performance of state farms and agencies in Xinjiang, *Bingtuan* in particular, during the mid-1970s was so poor, as is shown in the table, and posed such a heavy burden on the central government, that a decision was made by the central government in 1978 to dissolve *Bingtuan*, albeit this decision was later deemed to be a mistake and *Bingtuan* was restored to its original structure and status three years later in 1981 (Seymour 2000).

Xinjiang's dependency on the central government for subsidies and assistance continued during the post reform period even though its economic development was considered a success story in China during the 1990s when Xinjiang's GDP per capita, among the highest in the whole western region of China, was consistently above the national average (Goodman 2004, 6–9). This is because the relatively strong economic performance did not offset the rapidly increasing demand for financial expenditures in the region. For example, during the first twenty years of the reform, there was consistently a huge

Table 5.1 Government General Budgetary Revenue and Expenditure, Xinjiang and China, 1950–2015

	1	*2*	*3*	*4*	*5*	*6*
Year	*Revenue** *Xinjiang* *100 m. yuan*	*Expenditure^* *Xinjiang* *100 m. yuan*	*Balance/Rev* *Xinjiang* *%*	*Balance/Rev* *China* *%*	*Rev/GDP* *Xinjiang* *%*	*Rev/GDP* *China* *%*
1950	0.22	0.67	−204.54	−9.46	–#	–#
1955	1.73	1.83	−5.78	−7.16	14.05	27.4
1960	6.33	9.58	−51.34	−12.47	25.11	39.3
1965	4.53	4.89	−7.94	+2.82	18.72	27.6
1970	3.57	6.05	−69.46	+2.03	15.47	29.4
1975	1.01	8.85	−776.24	−0.64	3.59	27.2
1980	4.03	16.22	−302.48	−5.94	7.56	25.5
1985	8.47	28.60	−237.66	+0.03	7.54	22.2
1990	21.78	47.62	−118.64	−4.99	8.33	15.7
1995	38.28	96.40	−151.83	−9.31	4.69	10.3
2000	79.07	190.05	−140.36	−18.59	5.79	13.5
2005	180.32	519.02	−187.83	−7.21	6.92	17.3
2010	500.58	1,698.91	−239.39	−8.15	9.21	20.1
2015	1,330.85	3,804.87	−185.89	−15.5	14.27	22.1

Sources: Data for 1950–2005 are from *Statistical Collection of Sixty Years of New China*, data for 2010 and 2016 are from China and Xinjiang Statistics Yearbooks.
*It includes value-added, operation, and enterprise income taxes.
^It includes expenditures for agriculture, culture, education, science public health, administration, and subsidies to social security programs.
#Data not available.

gap between expenditure, which included both consumption and capital formation, and the regional GDP, with the former significantly outweighing the latter. The difference between the two amounted to at least 20 percent of Xinjiang's GDP and this shortfall was completely absorbed by the central government (Dreyer 2000; Sautman 2000). Indeed, during most of the 1990s and the year 2000, Xinjiang received either the very highest level or one of the highest levels of net financial transfers from the central government among its peer provincial level administrative units (Wiemer 2004, 175–176).

Table 5.1 lists Xinjiang's budgetary revenue and expenditures from 1950 until 2015. The table shows that there has been a significantly more severe imbalance between revenue and expenditures in Xinjiang, particularly since the reform, compared with China as a whole. The revenue/GDP ratio has been consistently much lower in Xinjiang than in China as a whole, indicating, as a general trend, Xinjiang's weaker financial base to engage in investment in social and human capital development and other social welfare-related services in the region. The shortfall in the budget, as is repeatedly observed by researchers, has been made up by the central government. Not only is there a shortage of funding, but the high level of volatility of the ratio of revenue over GDP for Xinjiang indicates that the funding available from the government is inconsistent from year to year in the region (Appleyard 2012; Caballero et al. 2012; Ferry et al. 2015).

THE ECONOMIC ASSISTANCE PROGRAM TO XINJIANG SINCE 2010

One of the most striking features of the 2010 Xinjiang assistance program is the phenomenal amount of financial resources that have been raised for this program. As was discussed in chapter 2, the 19 participating provinces and municipalities are asked to commit at least three-tenth percent of their respective yearly fiscal revenues to the development of the various administrative units that they have been matched with in the assistance program in Xinjiang.[3]

Consistent with missions of the assistance program implemented in Xinjiang during earlier times, there are pragmatic reasons for the institutionalized mass participation in the Xinjiang assistance program. By dividing up the burden of aid to Xinjiang among the various provinces and municipalities, the central government not only is able to drastically ease its own financial burden, but can also significantly increase both the volume and very likely the effectiveness of the assistance. Table 5.2 lists the amount of financial assistance committed by the 19 administrative units, based on the calculation of 0.3 percent of their budget revenues for the participating administrative units from 2010 to 2015.[4]

Table 5.2 Economic Aid to Xinjiang by Assistance Partner Units, 2010–2015, 100 Million Yuan

#	*Province/Municipality*	*2010*	*2011*	*2012*	*2013*	*2014*	*2015*
1	Guangdong Province	13.55	16.54	18.68	21.24	24.19	28.10
2	Shenzhen Municipality	3.32	4.02	4.44	5.19	6.24	8.18
3	Shanghai Municipality	8.62	10.29	11.23	12.33	13.75	16.56
4	Shandong Province	8.25	10.36	12.18	13.68	15.08	16.59
5	Beijing Municipality	7.06	9.02	9.94	10.98	12.08	14.17
6	Tianjin Municipality	3.20	4.36	5.28	6.23	7.17	8.00
7	Anhui Province	3.44	4.39	5.38	6.22	6.65	7.36
8	Zhejiang Province	7.82	9.45	10.32	11.39	12.36	14.43
9	Jiangsu Province	12.24	15.44	17.58	19.7	21.7	24.08
10	Liaoning Province	6.01	7.93	9.31	10.03	9.58	6.38
11	Heilongjiang Province	2.26	2.99	3.49	3.83	3.90	3.49
12	Jiangxi Province	2.33	3.16	4.11	4.86	5.64	6.49
13	Hebei Province	3.99	5.21	6.25	6.88	7.34	7.94
14	Shanxi Province	2.91	3.64	4.55	5.10	5.46	4.92
15	Fujian Province	3.45	4.50	5.32	6.35	7.08	7.63
16	Hunan Province	3.24	4.55	5.34	6.09	6.78	7.54
17	Hubei Province	3.33	4.58	5.47	6.57	7.70	9.01
18	Henan Province	4.14	5.16	6.12	7.24	8.21	9.04
19	Jilin Province	1.80	2.55	3.12	3.47	3.61	3.69
	Total	106.25	137.09	156.31	176.56	194.37	214.1

Source: China Statistics Yearbook 2016, Table 3–9.

According to the table, the largest amount of financial assistance is provided by Guangdong Province, which is matched with Kashgar region, with 13.55 hundred million yuan in 2010 and then more than doubling that with more than 28 hundred million yuan in 2015. The next highest amount is provided by Jiangsu Province (assistant deliverer for Yili District and part of Kizilsu Prefecture) with more than 12 hundred million yuan in 2010 and twice as much in 2015, followed by Shanghai, Shandong, and Zhejiang. All these provinces or cities with the highest volumes of economic aid to Xinjiang are located in the coastal region of China and all of them have been assigned to assist southern Xinjiang, at least partially.

The table also shows that the total amount of financial resources provided by all the 19 assisting units amounted to more than 10 billion yuan in 2010 and this figure gradually increased over the years, reaching 21.4 billion yuan in 2015.

There are consistent patterns in the way the economic and financial assistance to Xinjiang by the partnership administrative units is delivered and utilized. The single most highlighted aspect that receives funding is manufacturing industries (*chanye yuanjiang*). Furthermore, with hardly any exception, the most common investment strategy to stimulate industrial and manufacturing production by nearly all the administrative units has been to develop industrial and technological parks or zones throughout Xinjiang (Xinjiang Yearbooks since 2010, section on assistance program).

INDUSTRIAL AND TECHNOLOGICAL PARKS BUILT WITH RESOURCES OF ASSISTANCE PROGRAM

The construction of industrial and technological parks is significant hallmarks in the economic development in China since the reform. Initially they were only allowed to be built in the coastal areas. It was not until the 1990s that other regions had the permission to build them. As a result, industrial and technological parks have mushroomed throughout China with the total number reaching thousands (Shi et al. 2012). Normally, when a piece of land is designated as the site of an industrial park within an administrative area such as a city or a county, it receives accommodations for the construction of facilities and infrastructure necessary for industrial production. In addition, the park management or local government often offers incentives or preferential treatment, such as tax rebates or other government subsidies, to companies and businesses for their investment in industrial parks or zones. Consequently, spaces in industrial parks are often actively sought after by businesses and companies, especially in the coastal region, that have attracted investors not only within China but all over the world.

Prior to 2010, only the two major cities, Urumqi and Shihezi, in Xinjiang had industrial and technological development zones or parks. The 2010 assistance program has drastically changed this situation. Currently nearly all cities and counties in Xinjiang have constructed, or are in the process of constructing, industrial parks. Let us use Hotan, the economically most disadvantaged district with the lowest level of industrialization in Xinjiang, as is shown in Table 5.3, as an example. As is reported in Xinjiang yearbooks since 2011, at least one industrial or technological park has been constructed in every one of all the seven counties within the jurisdiction of the district as well as in the City of Hotan within the last several years. As a matter of fact, in the county of Pishan in Hotan District, assisted by both Anhui Province and Beijing Municipality, there are as many as three industrial parks or technological zones: Anhui Comprehensive Economic and Technological Development Zone in Pishan (皮山县安徽综合经济技术开发区), Pishan Industrial Park (皮山县工业园) and Pishan-Moyu (P-M) Industrial Park (皮墨工业园区), with the last one being affiliated with XPCC.[5]

Not only is there a multitude and wide spread distribution of industrial parks and technological zones in Xinjiang, but some of them are so elaborate and extensive that they are divided into various subzones or subparks. The Aksu Industrial Park in the city of Aksu built with the aid of Zhejiang Province, for example, is made up of three parts that are named, respectively, the Southern Park (南园), the Western Park (西园) and Zhejiang Taizhou Industrial Park (浙江台州产业园).

Adequate funding and speedy construction of facilities are only part of the story of active operations of industrial parks and technological zones. Since the main purpose of assembling these constructions and infrastructure is to facilitate industrial and commercial activities in local areas, attracting business investment to utilize the facilities is therefore essential to ensuring the successful functionality of the industrial parks. In this regard, Xinjiang's experience seems different from other parts of China, particularly the coastal region. While it is very often competitive to obtain spaces in industrial parks in the coastal area, as was discussed above, it is apparently a challenge to find businesses that are interested in investing in Xinjiang, especially remote areas of Xinjiang.

All participating provinces and municipalities in the assistance program have been making, or probably were asked to make, aggressive efforts to lure businesses to invest in industrial parks in Xinjiang. It is reported that the provincial government of Liaoning, assigned to assist the city of Tacheng in Yli Kazak Autonomous Prefecture, "required that every city in the province would arrange to have three or four or even more relatively large industrial projects to invest in Xinjiang" in 2011 (Xinjiang Yearbook 2011, 155). The following year, Liaoning government held a conference with the

Table 5.3 Economic Indicators of Prefecture-Level Administrative Units in Xinjiang, 2014

	Total GDP	*FirstSec*	*SecondSec*	*ThirdSec*	*Industry*	*Average GDP*
	10000 yuan	%	%	%	%	*Yuan*
Urumqi	24,614,698	1.14	36.81	62.07	31.13	70,428
Kalamay	8,476,725	0.61	75.48	23.90	82.04	153,084
Shihezi	2,928,469	3.54	59.23	37.22	45.73	81,370
Turpan	2,600,194	16.23	53.83	29.94	47.42	40,457
Hami	4,021,829	9.45	56.06	34.48	38.41	65,646
Changji	1,060,874	22.72	48.79	28.48	39.60	66,005
Yli	15,620,784	27.41	34.17	38.42	24.24	32,825
Tacheng	5,941,184	34.87	34.43	30.69	25.37	44,851
Altay	2,256,160	1.92	45.01	35.73	33.64	35,932
Bortala	2,581,125	24.02	27.66	48.39	17.69	52,448
Bayingol	11,187,864	16.51	61.16	22.32	55.11	79,055
Aksu	7,498,888	29.41	31.65	38.92	22.89	29,293
Kizilsu	892,437	14.68	32.11	53.19	19.11	15,222
Kashgar	6,884,030	29.99	30.53	39.47	17.30	16,024
Hotan	1,984,208	29.53	17.64	52.82	6.43	8,993

Xinjiang Statistics Yearbook 2015.

14 prefecture-level cities within the province concerning their participation in the assistance program. At the conference, an agreement was reached to divide up the workload and funds associated with the Xinjiang assistance program during the twelfth five-year plan period (2011–2015). Leaders of the 14 cities signed contracts concerning responsibilities for their respective share of the package that involved 180 industrial projects and twenty billion yuan investment fund for the Xinjiang assistance program during this time frame (Xinjiang Yearbook 2012, 125).

The Beijing government has also been heavily involved in efforts to channel investment from Beijing to Xinjiang. As soon as Beijing was assigned to assist Hotan in 2010, the Beijing government arranged to have more than 70 key industrial companies from Beijing to visit and consider investing in Hotan. Beijing also established a specifically designated fund for assistance to Hotan and asked businesses, companies, organizations, and other agencies to make donations to the fund (Xinjiang Yearbook 2011, 43).

In addition to measures to fund, construct and utilize industrial facilities in Xinjiang, the concerted efforts made by the leadership of participating units also included tour trips to Xinjiang, meetings between potential investors from both inland and coastal China and local governmental officials and other relevant individuals in Xinjiang, as well as introduction sessions to local conditions and culture. Based again on yearbooks, the various outreach measures seem to be effective in enticing investment in Xinjiang, as the case of Hotan's development illustrates. With the money generated through the fundraising efforts described above, Beijing utilized the strategy of investment and financing to engage in projects that facilitate production facilities and activities for the local economy, which include greenhouse construction, development of materials and technologies to prevent desertification, production of herbal medicine, processing of dry fruits and other local agricultural products, among others (Xinjiang Yearbook 2011, 43).

PROJECTS AND ACTIVITIES IN INDUSTRIAL PARKS

Beijing's strategy of stimulating industrial development is typical among participants in the assistance program. Indeed, the focus on the processing of local products and utilizing local conditions and natural resources are among the dominant patterns of investment strategies in the assistance program. Guangdong's 580 million yuan investment in a textile plant with an anticipated production capacity of 200 thousand spun of cotton yarn in Jiashi County of Kashgar District is another example. The decision to set up the textile factory was based on the fact that cotton is one of the major agricultural products in southern Xinjiang and that Division 3 of *Bingtuan*, which is matched with Guangdong in the assistance program, is one of the major cotton producing units within *Bingtuan* and in Xinjiang as well (Xinjiang Yearbook 2011, 47).

In addition to manufacturing industries to process agricultural products, there are also the construction of heavy industrial facilities, and these industries have been taking place at a vast scale that Xinjiang has never seen before. For example, several provinces and municipalities have helped build cement factories in Xinjiang, with the largest one built by Shandong Province in Kashgar in 2010. Other cement plants include one built by Shanghai in Shache, also in Kashgar; the HengXing 恒星 Cement Factory with a daily productivity capacity of 4,000 tons in Tacheng area; the Western Cement Factory by Tianjin Municipality in Yutian County of Hotan District and the Yaobai Cement Project (尧柏水泥项目) also in Hotan (Xinjiang yearbooks 2011 to 2015).

Other industries built with resources from the assistance program include chemical plants, production for construction materials, mineral extraction and production, paper and energy production, coal mining and processing and iron and steel plants. The single largest industrial project in terms of total investment volume in the whole assistance program as of 2016 is the Ganxin Iron and Steel Project 赣鑫钢铁项目in the Heavy Industry Park in the city of Atushi of Kizilsu Kyrgiz Autonomous Region in southern Xinjiang. With the total planned investment volume of 7.5 billion yuan and anticipated annual production of 3 million tons of high strength steel, the project, with assistance from Jiangxi Province in southern China, is scheduled to be completed in three stages. The groundbreaking ceremony for the first stage took place on September 2, 2010. With an anticipated investment volume of 2.5 billion yuan, the first stage of the project was expected to generate an annual sale value of 3.2 billion yuan, a profit of 720 million yuan, a tax revenue of 280 million yuan as well as 2000 jobs for the local region (Xinjiang Yeabook 2011, 45).

Jiangxi Province is by no means economically advanced among all the assistance-providing units. Actually, the financial assistance provided by Jiangxi (233 million yuan in 2010 and 649 million yuan in 2015) is among the lowest in all the provinces and municipalities involved in the assistance program, as is shown in Table 5.2. This is probably the reason that Jiangxi is matched with only one county, the county of Akto, in Kizilsu Kyrgiz Autonomous Prefecture while Jiangsu Province is assigned to assist all other areas of Kizilsu prefecture including the city of Atushi and the two additional counties in the prefecture: the counties of Akqi and Wuqia.

Similarly, Kizilsu Kyrgyz Autonomous Prefecture is one of the most underdeveloped areas in Xinjiang, as is shown in Table 5.3. According to the table, Kizilsu's economy is the smallest among all the prefecture-level units in Xinjiang measured in terms of total GDP volumes. Furthermore, the proportions of industrial economic sector in relation to the total economy in

Kizilsu is also among the lowest in comparison to other administrative units in Xinjiang. Only less than one-fifth (19 percent) of the economy was for industrial production in Kizilsu in 2014. Finally, the average GDP of Kizilsu is second lowest in the region, next only to Hotan, which makes it one of the poorest districts in Xinjiang. All these indicators suggest that Kizilsu does not have a strong foundation for industrial development, let alone the development of a massive facility of an iron and steel plant. In addition, located in the most western end of Xinjiang, Kizilsu is one of the most remote areas in Xinjiang and in China as well, as was commented by the renowned Swedish scholar/diplomat Gunnar Jarring who had attempted eagerly to visit the area when he was in Kashgar, the neighboring town to Akto, in both the 1930s and 1980s, but had failed both times. Among the various reasons for the two equally disappointing situations for Jarring that were half a century apart was its remoteness and difficulties of its accessibility (Jarring 1986).

Given all these circumstances, the intriguing question is this: Why is the single largest project, in terms of invest cost, in the Xinjiang assistance program constructed in Kizilsu? The following statements by official media sheds light on this issue:

> There are abundant deposits of mineral resources in Kezhou (Kizilsu Prefecture, note added by this author) area, particularly iron and nonferrous metals. The already identified 69 types of minerals discovered in the area make up 40.35 percent of these types of minerals found in China. The steel plant in Kezhou can operate by utilizing exclusively (100 percent) iron ore that is produced locally.
>
> In addition, there are other advantages of building the steel plant in Kezhou. There are two class-one level border port posts in the area: Tuerga吐尔尕特 and Ilkestan 伊尔克什坦. Furthermore, there is no other steel plant within the 1,500 kilometer radius of the city. None of the countries across the border from Kezhou, i.e., Kyrgystan, Tajikstan, Afghanistan and Pakistan, have steel plant facilities. Consequently, there is a huge market potential for the plant in Kezhou. It could be the "bridgehead" (qiaotoubao—added by the author)[6] of the export of iron and steel from China to the four countries in Central Asia. (TianshanNet 2010)

Having stated the above, however, it is curious that there does not seem to be any news circulation or updates concerning Ganxin Iron and Steel Project since June 2012. In the official annual publication of Xinjiang Yearbook, there is a specifically designated section on status and changes of projects associated with the assistance program. Both the 2011 and 2012 editions of the yearbook discuss the Ganxin Iron and Steel Plant. However, it has not been mentioned since 2013. Similar outcome has resulted from an online search. The most recent online news report that I could find about the Kezhou steel plant was dated June 6, 2012, and it says that the plant was still in the preparation stage but it would soon be under construction and start producing steel by July 2013 (Langegangtie 兰格钢铁网 2012/06/06).

SUMMARY

The rich deposits of natural resources in Xinjiang would be essential ingredients for successful industrial development. But Xinjiang's economy, particularly industrial economy, has remained underdeveloped. The Chinese governments over thousands of years have adopted various strategies to cope with problems associated with the underdeveloped economy of the region. Migrants who are sent to Xinjiang are expected to be self-dependent economically, for example, instead of relying on external assistance. However, the rulers of China, particularly the CCP, have to provide substantial financial assistance to Xinjiang whenever there are revenue shortages in the region, which are frequent occurrences.

The two different patterns of economic dynamics—relying on external financial aid vs. developing self-sustainable local economy—have drastically different consequences, which the central government and assistance-providing units are fully aware of. They refer to the two approaches as "blood-transfusion" and "blood-making," respectively. Even though the approach of blood-making is believed to produce the optimal outcome, the economic assistance provided to Xinjiang since 2010 is nonetheless heavily based on the blood transfusion model: Strategies and experiences of industrial economic development in the coastal region have been intensively applied to Xinjiang. The construction of industrial and technological parks and zones as the dominant pattern of economic development throughout Xinjiang in recent years is an illustration of this phenomenon.

It remains to be seen whether the approach of transplanting the economic development model of the coastal region to Xinjiang will generate consequences anticipated by the central government and assistance-providing units. In the field of education, however, there is much less ambiguity in terms of changes and consequences brought about by the assistance program. These changes may become reasons for enhanced racial tension in Xinjiang, as will be discussed in the next chapter.

NOTES

1. Taiwan, which became officially part of China in 1885, was another controversial region within the court for similar reasons (Perdue 2005, 426–427).

2. Please see previous chapter for the discussion concerning Qing policies on Han migration to Xinjiang.

3. It is probably more accurate to say that the participating units have been demanded or forced by the central government to make the pledge (Halper 2012, 161–162).

4. The figures presented in this table are most likely the lowest values of economic assistance to Xinjiang by participating provinces and cities for the indicated years.

There are two reasons for this statement. One is that all the figures in the table are calculated based on 0.3 percent revenues of the provinces and cities. But the expected economic aid to Xinjiang is a range of percentage points (0.3–0.6 percent) of revenues of the provinces and cities (Szadziewski 2011, 107).The other reason is that the figures are based on general budgetary revenues instead of total revenues that would include tax revenues as well. For example, in 2015, the general public budget revenue for Beijing was 472.38 billion yuan and the tax revenue was 426.3 billion yuan. The figure in Table 5.2 is based on the .03 percent of the former revenue only. This is also how figures for all other provinces and municipalities have been calculated.

5. The P-M Industrial Park, constructed with aid from Beijing, sits near the 224 Regiment of the 14th Division of XPCC, which is located between Pishan and Moyu Counties. Under the jurisdiction of the XPCC and with XPCC provincial level status, the Park was first built on a piece of land measuring 3.11 square kilometers in 2011. It was then expanded to cover 15.08 square kilometers in 2013 with the investment of 27 companies by that year (XPCC Statistics Bureau 2015).

6. Let me quote Miller's excellent explanation of the phrase "bridgehead" in the context of discussion of official documents in China: "'Bridgehead' is a military term referring to a fortress controlling the frontline, but Beijing's strategists have adopted it to describe a regional gateway or geostrategic hub. The term frequently appears in government reports, but is not directly translated into foreign languages, suggesting the planners are aware of its unsettling connotations" (Miller 2017, 98).

Chapter 6

Educational Assistance to Xinjiang

Education is one of the institutions that are designated to receive a disproportionately large share of resources provided by the assistance program in Xinjiang since 2010. More than half (52.5 percent) of the total volume of 11.17 billion yuan provided by the assistance program in 2013 was devoted to education (Xinjiang Yearbook 2014, 109–110). The total amount of funds devoted to education increased drastically from 2.895 billion yuan in 2012 to 5.873 billion yuan in 2013 and then to 12.12 billion yuan in 2014 (Xinjiang Yearbook 2013, 120; 2014, 110; 2015, 133). Not only was there a dramatic increase in the total funds, but the proportion of financial commitment to education also increased significantly. In 2011, the total budget of the assistance program for the five-year period of 2011–2015 was set to be 63.91 billion yuan with 13.75 percent (8.79 billion yuan) committed to education assistance. In 2012, the total assistance budget for the same five-year period was readjusted to be 63.94 billion yuan, and the amount for educational assistance was raised to 9.77 billion yuan, which constituted 15.26 percent of the total five-year budget (Xinjiang Yearbook 2012, 152; 2013, 120).

However, not all aspects of education were equally treated in terms of receiving funding. Bilingual education, which is one of the most controversial issues in China's ethnic policies, seems to be the most prioritized, receiving 69 percent and 63 percent of all education-related funding from the assistance program in 2011 and 2012, respectively (Xinjiang Yearbook 2012, 152; 2013, 120).

The heavy emphasis on bilingual education in the assistance program reflects recent orientations of ethnic relations and policies in China. Researchers have repeatedly argued that the institution of education should never be treated simply as a mechanism to enhance and transform knowledge. It must always be viewed as part of an integrated system to help maintain and reinforce the social order established by dominant forces in the society (Desjardins 2015a and 2015b; Leibold and Chen 2014). Desjardins states:

> Thus the idea that education can simply be taken at face value to be empowering, or serve an enlightening and even transformative function is perhaps too optimistic. Primarily because it neglects the conditioning effects of power relations and the fact that education has important effects on the position of citizens in any prevailing hierarchy of social relations. It also neglects the reproductive forces associated with education, namely those that seek to preserve or even enhance dominant interests. (Desjardins 2015b, 240)

China has been engaged in campaigns to raise its status and spread its influence in the global arena. The affairs of Xinjiang will play a decisive role in the realization of China's ambitious strategic agenda, as was discussed in earlier chapters. What has been, and what continues to be, transformed in Xinjiang's educational system, particularly changes in language policies, will produce fundamental and far-reaching social, political, and economic consequences in both Xinjiang and China as a whole. These changes will also shape China's international relations and affairs.

Before addressing the impact of language policies on Xinjiang and China, it is necessary to review how China's shifting political and economic orientations have influenced language policies in Xinjiang. In other words, there is a two-way relationship between educational policies and social and economic structures in Xinjiang and China. As one scholar points out, in PRC, "language is above all else a political tool" (Schluessel 2007, 254).

LANGUAGE REFORM IN XINJIANG

Several waves of language reform have taken place in Xinjiang since the founding of the PRC. The most well-known are probably the numerous and arbitrary changes of the alphabet of ethnic minority languages. All these changes were pushed from top authorities based on either China's foreign policy considerations or nation-building motivations, or both (Dwyer 2004). Take the language of the largest ethnic group in Xinjiang, the Uyghur, as an example. Traditionally, Uyghur language for the Uyghur and many other Turkic-speaking populations in Xinjiang was based on Arabic script, which was near and dear to the Turkic people and culture in Xinjiang, as Dwyer points out:

> Nearly all Uyghurs favor the Arabic script for reasons of practicality, aesthetics, and group identity. Knowledge of this script allows access to the largest body

of modern Uyghur and premodern Central Asian literature. The Arabic script is considered by Uyghurs to be beautiful; indeed, it is also an important art form. (Dwyer 2004, 19)

Shortly after the founding of the PRC, however, a decision was made to change the Arabic Uyghur script to Cyrillic alphabet. The major reason for this change was to show China's solidarity with the former Soviet Union, with whom China was on friendly relations at the time. By adopting the Cyrillic script, which was used in the Soviet educational system, China was obviously making a gesture to enhance its ties with the USSR (Rhoads, et al. 2014). Besides, by making this change, Xinjiang could make convenient use of teaching materials imported from across the border.

As could be expected, the ideologically and politically driven policy was subject to uncertainties and inconsistencies. Within just a few years, the relationship between the two countries deteriorated, resulting in Xinjiang's engagement in yet another round of Uyghur language reform. In 1958, Uyghur Cyrillic script was changed again, this time to a Latin-based transliteration similar to the phonetic pin yin spelling of Chinese characters. This policy change was part of the governmental efforts to pave the way for China to create an official *lingua franca* based on the dominant Mandarin language. Not surprisingly, this forcefully imposed Cyrillic alphabet never gained popularity among the Uyghur population even though it had been in use for nearly three decades. When it was finally abandoned in 1984, the traditional Uyghur Arabic Script was readopted (Wang, P. 2016).

The decision to return to the Uyghur Arabic Script was certainly a welcome move among the Uyghur and numerous other Turkic populations in Xinjiang. However, the repeated changes in the script of the Uyghur language since the 1950s have resulted in the unfortunate phenomenon that generations of Uyghur and other Turkic students were not exposed to the same language script. The discontinuity of the traditional Arabic script highly valued by the local population resulted in a severe interruption to the culture, heritage, tradition, and identity of the Uyghur and other Turkic populations in Xinjiang and elsewhere (Dwyer 2004). Research has reported that the Uyghur and other ethnic minority populations have expressed strong feelings that the decades-long interruption to the Arabic Uyghur script was actually an intended manipulation by the Chinese government to generate intergenerational discontinuity in terms of Uyghur culture, history and identity (Benson 2004, 197). Whether or not the discontinuity of the use of Arabic script was a result of premeditated calculation is a controversial issue, but what is clear is that it has indeed resulted in the consequence of cutting off older Uyghur generations from the younger ones, or vice versa, in terms of their culture, tradition and heritage (Dwyer 2004).

In addition to arbitrary changes of the alphabet of minority languages, other changes and reforms have been taking place in Xinjiang's education as well. The most significant of these changes is institutionalized and increasingly intensified efforts to integrate minority languages and the Han Mandarin language, namely, bilingual education. The purpose of bilingual education in China is, in theory, to keep a balance to China's multiethnic and multicultural geo-entity, maintain social harmony, strengthen societal integration, and enhance nation-building (Leibold and Chen 2014; Ma 2015). But, as the discussion below will demonstrate, the push for bilingual education in Xinjiang in recent years has been proceeding so aggressively that it seems to be in the process of practically eliminating minority languages as both the academic discipline and teaching medium. Indeed, the drastic downplay of minority languages in Xinjiang's educational system in recent years, which is facilitated by the assistance program, is a sharp departure from historical patterns of educational policies concerning Han and minority language teaching in Xinjiang.

BILINGUAL EDUCATION IN XINJIANG AND CHINA: A BRIEF HISTORY

When discussing bilingual education in Xinjiang, and in China as a whole, a note of clarification is necessary. As researchers have pointed out, the concept of "bilingual education" in China should not be construed in the light of the face value of the expression, at least not according to its definition in the literature on the Western educational system. In the West, bilingual education normally refers to the approach of using two languages in a parallel fashion in teaching, or, more commonly, the situation whereby the mother tongue (i.e., ethnic minority) language receives primary attention while a second language is introduced to the students.

In China, bilingual education usually refers to the promotion of Mandarin as the language of instruction. In this process, the minority mother tongue language is often used as the transitional tool preparing students to ultimately receive lessons solely in Mandarin language. As can be imagined, as a result of the continued implementation of bilingual education operated under such a model, the Chinese Mandarin language plays an increasingly more prominent role in the educational systems of ethnic minority areas. Over time, Mandarin would become either the dominant or sole language of instruction in the curriculum of ethnic minority students (He 2014, 62; Schluessel 2007, 256–257), which has become the pattern in nearly all ethnic minority areas in China (He 2014). In Xinjiang, this process has been significantly hastened and made all the more drastic by the recent version of the assistance program starting from 2010.

China currently implements a nine-year mandatory education system, which will be changed to 12 years by 2020 (Postiglione 2014, 32). In Xinjiang, the following seven teaching languages are used in primary and secondary school systems: Mandarin, Uyghur (which is used by not only the Uyghur, but also Uzbek, Tartar, and Tajik populations), Kazakh, Kirgiz, Mongolian, Xibo, and Russian. Three of them are also used in tertiary education: Mandarin, Uyghur, and Kazakh (Simayi 2014, 136).

Ever since Mandarin (Putonghua) was designated as the official spoken language under Emperor Daoguang of the Qing Dynasty in 1845 (He 2014, 53), it has been a controversial issue how to balance the use of official language and aboriginal languages in frontier areas primarily inhabited by ethnic minority populations. Chinese rulers have adopted various approaches regarding this matter. With the practice of a mostly autonomy system, "the Qing used the Tibetan language to rule over Tibet, the Uyghur language to rule in Xinjiang, and Mongolian in Mongol areas" (He 2014, 48).

The earliest efforts to aggressively insert the influence of Chinese language in the educational system of non-Han ethnic populations in Xinjiang could be traced to the beginning of the last century (Simayi 2014, 136). The first governor of Xinjiang representing the Nationalist government, Yang Zengxin (in office 1912–1928), pushed for teaching Mandarin in schools while banning other languages such as Russian. But since only about five percent of Xinjiang's population was of Han ethnicity at the time and there were very limited educational resources for Mandarin teaching, the campaign to introduce Mandarin language into the educational system was therefore not very successful. Furthermore, it was a bit absurd to try to teach Mandarin to students in Xinjiang since Mandarin language did not enjoy much popularity in the war-torn China at that time. The only logical reason that may help explain Yang's motive to promote Mandarin language teaching in Xinjiang was that it was part of the government's plans to control the region and infiltrate the Han influence among the majority of the populations in the region who were non-Han and did not speak Mandarin (Schluessel 2007, 252–253).

There was not much consistency, however, in the government's practice on Mandarin language teaching during the Nationalist rule. When the Soviet Union replaced China as having a more significant influence on Xinjiang during the 1930s and 1940s, Xinjiang's education curriculum followed more closely the Soviet educational model, which emphasized native-language education and ethnic participation in education (Schluessel 2007, 252–253). Mandarin was still taught to students of non-Han ethnic groups, but the educational system advocated using native languages of various ethnic groups as teaching languages. Furthermore, non-Han and non-Uyghur students were given an option to choose either Uyghur or Mandarin in addition to focusing on their mother tongue languages at school (Schluessel 2007, 253–254).

Indeed, the governor of Xinjiang toward the end of the Nationalist period, that is, Sheng Shicai (in office 1933–1944), was known to value education, especially education of various ethnic populations. Under his rule, education, including that of minority populations, experienced rapid development in Xinjiang (Benson 2004, 193–194).[1]

BILINGUAL EDUCATION IN XINJIANG: PRC ERA

Compared with its predecessors, the PRC government has been much more aggressive in inserting Mandarin language into the educational system of minority regions. Bilingual education in Xinjiang was initiated during the early 1950s and has developed rapidly since then. In the early years of the PRC, a relatively liberal approach was adopted to let students choose either Mandarin or Russian as the second language. During the late 1960s and most of 1970s, however, minority language education suffered severe setbacks. Uyghur language was not taught at all during those years, even in schools located in Uyghur areas (Wang, P. 2016). But, starting from the end of the 1970s, there was a relatively open atmosphere in which minority populations had the freedom to pursue their language, culture and religion, and this trend continued into the 1980s. Institutional changes during the early stage of the reform period, such as the State Constitution adopted in 1982 and Law on Regional Autonomy passed in 1984, played positive roles in enhancing minority education by, among other things, introducing affirmative action programs in order to enhance the status of native languages of ethnic populations (Simayi 2014).

For the most part, two types of schools existed in Xinjiang prior to the 1980s. These were schools with the minority mother tongue language as the teaching medium and those that used Mandarin as the medium. Not surprisingly, most minority children attended the former and most Chinese students attended the latter type of schools. Even though the two types of schools and classes were segregated, Mandarin was taught as a second language in minority language schools and minority languages taught in Chinese schools. The relatively balanced and diverse educational approaches played crucial and positive roles in both the social and economic development of the region. For example, just as functional as Chinese schools, Uyghur schools contributed significantly in raising Uyghur people's educational level and in training scientists, teachers and other professionals in Xinjiang and beyond. Indeed, as Wang points out that during the early decades of the PRC, "the Uyghurs had a sound Uyghur language-based education system from elementary schools to 4-year universities and produced many high-ranking and well-known scholars, professionals and government officials who are serving in various fields today both domestically and internationally" (Wang, P. 2016, 91).

Starting from the mid- to late 1980s, there has been a gradual shift of the pattern of language teaching and requirements in Xinjiang with the Uyghur and other minority languages slowly losing their prominence and Mandarin rapidly gaining its influence. Prior to the 1980s, non-Han children did not have to start learning Mandarin until middle school, which meant that the majority of non-Han students learned nearly all subjects that were taught in school in their mother tongue languages. But since 1984, Xinjiang Educational Commission required that Mandarin become a mandatory requirement starting from third grade and this requirement was further pushed earlier to first grade by the 2000s. Meanwhile, Mandarin became the language of instruction for an increasing number of subjects starting from the 1990s. Dwyer points out that in ethnic minority classes and schools, "it is the minority language (e.g., Uyghur) that is taught as if it were a second language" (Dwyer 2004, 39). Since the mid-2000s, there have been systematic efforts to change curricular and schools that were originally independent minority-language-based to either bilingual or totally Mandarin-based. In other words, independent minority language schools were gradually eliminated (Schluessel 2007, 257–258). "In 2005, the regional language committee directed almost all schools throughout Xinjiang to use Mandarin as the language of instruction" (Wang, P. 2016, 92).

Numerous researchers have questioned the rationale and justification that Mandarin has become a mandatory language requirement for ethnic minority students but Han students do not have to learn minority languages, not even in areas where the Han is the demographic minority, such as Xinjiang (e.g., Dwyer 2004; Tsung 2014; He 2014). More importantly, and not surprisingly, research has shown that minority populations are resentful of the language policies discussed above.[2] Some researchers suggest that China's language policies are responsible for much of the oppositions and antagonistic sentiment of minority populations toward the Han in Xinjiang because these policies constantly force minorities to reconfigure their ethnic identities (e.g., Dwyer 2004). Others argue that the notion of language rights (LR) as part of cultural rights needs to be brought into the discourse concerning language policies in Xinjiang (e.g., Wang, P. 2016). Still others view China's language policies, as they are implemented in Xinjiang, as severe violations of not only language and cultural rights, but fundamental human rights. One researcher even calls for international intervention in order to prevent the Uyghur language from becoming one of the dead languages as a result of the Chinese government's policies (Bewicke 2009).

The increasing level of the Mandarin requirement and the gradual reduction of minority language requirement in the educational system have been taking place with several distinctive patterns. While there has been a constant intensification of Mandarin requirement over time in all types of educational institutions, these changes first took place at the tertiary educational level, then high school, middle school and finally elementary school levels. In recent years, Chinese has been taught in pre-school education as well. In terms of geographic locations, schools in northern Xinjiang, such as Urumqi, Tacheng and Turpan, saw these changes taking place before those in southern Xinjiang. Furthermore, the changes occurred initially in urban areas and are now gradually spreading to rural areas and nomadic communities (Simayi 2014).

Xinjiang University, which was founded in 1949 as a bilingual institution, was the very first institution in Xinjiang to experience the Uyghur language restriction. During the last century, Uyghur students at Xinjiang University were taught nearly all subjects with Uyghur language as the teaching medium. However, it was decided by the Xinjiang Education Commission that starting from September 2002, Xinjiang University would no longer offer courses in Uyghur language. Dwyer comments in her article published in 2004 "Now even Uyghur is taught entirely in Chinese; only for Chagatay (Middle Turkic) poetry is the use of Uyghur in the classroom allowed" (Dwyer 2004, 39–40). Besides, there were no Uyghur textbooks available any more, all textbooks used at the University are written in Chinese. In order to facilitate the rigorous Mandarin language requirement, minority students were required to take a Chinese language qualification test after one-year intensive Chinese language study at the university.

Meanwhile, plans were made to eventually eliminate the one-year Mandarin preparatory courses for minority students at Xinjiang's universities (Tsung 2014, 147). It was decided that the most effective mechanism to achieve this goal would be to enhance Mandarin and downsize minority languages as the teaching medium for primary and secondary education until the latter would be phased out and replaced by the former. This is the reason for the aggressive campaigns to enhance "bilingual education" facilitated by the assistance program instituted in 2010.

BILINGUAL EDUCATION UNDER THE ASSISTANCE PROGRAM IN XINJIANG

The development of Xinjiang's bilingual education can be divided into three stages. The first stage, which lasted for several decades starting from the beginning of the PRC, introduced several hours of Mandarin per week to minority students. The second stage started in 1992 and it required that science-related courses be taught in Mandarin while other subjects were still delivered in minority languages. The beginning of the 21st century saw the change to the third stage, which is a drastically different model whereby minority students are expected to be taught all subjects in Mandarin language only (Tsung 2014, 145–148).

As can be imagined, it cannot possibly be an easy task to implement this radical and ambitious educational policy. Among the many challenges, the one that demands the most immediate attention is the staffing issue, as is repeatedly mentioned by researchers (Tsung 2014; Simayi 2014, 148). Hiring and maintaining qualified bilingual teachers are difficult, particularly in southern Xinjiang and in schools in rural areas of southern Xinjiang (Tsung 2014). The following statements by a principal of a rural school in southern Xinjiang, reported by Tsung in her research (2014), vividly illustrate the seriousness of the problem of the shortage of teachers of Chinese language, at least in rural southern Xinjiang: "We used to start the Chinese class from Year 4. Now the government asks schools to start teaching Chinese from Year 3, but no teachers are available. I have problems in keeping good Chinese teachers here. A number of Han Chinese teachers were assigned to our school before, but they all left. They could not speak Uyghur and did not talk to other teachers. They could not explain things in Uyghur to students, which was hard for the students. They did not want to teach in the local school, they wanted to go to a large city" (Tsung 2014, 173).[3]

Not surprisingly, the training of bilingual teachers is treated as the most pressing issue for the educational assistance program to Xinjiang since 2010. According to the official report in Xinjiang Yearbooks, as many as 37,200 teachers received bilingual education training provided by the assistance program from 2010 to 2013 (Xinjiang Yearbook 2014, 110). The majority of the trainees, about 61 percent, were in training for less than a week, another 21 percent had received training lasting from one week to three months, and the remaining teachers (18 percent) had enrolled in training sessions with a time frame of minimally half-a year to up to two years. Most of the training took place in Xinjiang but about a quarter (22.3 percent) of the trainees were sent away to receive training in facilities in assistance providing areas (Xinjiang Yearbook 2014, 110). For example, Jishou （吉首）University set up a Xinjiang Bilingual Teachers Training Center on its campus in Xiangxi （湘西）Autonomous Prefecture of Hunan Province in southern China. Seventy bilingual teachers from Turpan Prefecture received training at this facility in 2012 alone (Xinjiang Yearbook 2013, 130).

It is an expensive endeavor to train teachers, especially large numbers of them. The average cost for training one bilingual teacher in Xinjiang was 5,953 yuan in 2013. Based on the total number of teachers who received training that year, more than 221 million yuan was spent training bilingual teachers and the expense was all paid for by the assistance delivering units (Xinjiang Yearbook 2014, 110). This was a substantial amount of money considering that the average annual income for rural residents in Xinjiang in 2013 was 7,296 yuan (Xinjiang Statistical Yearbook 2015, 22–23).[4]

The actual figure for training teachers probably varied from one assistance providing unit to another and, as a general rule, it has been increasing over the years. Economically more advanced areas probably could afford more for this course than other areas. For example, it is reported that Shanghai increased the average budget of training each teacher to 11,500 yuan in 2014 (Yearbook 2015, 134), which was almost double the average amount for training each teacher for Xinjiang as a whole during the previous year.

In addition to training teachers, other approaches have been pursued as well for educational assistance to Xinjiang. Programs of student exchange are examples of such a pursuit. Fourteen higher educational institutions in Hunan Province admitted a total of 122 high school graduates from Turpan in 2011 (Xinjiang Yearbook 2012, 159). Henan Province recruited 603 unemployed college graduates in Xinjiang to attend training provided by 15 universities in Henan Province in 2013 (Xinjiang Yearbook 2014, 119). In addition to attending university education, there are even more exchange programs for vocational training for local middle and high school students in Xinjiang. Heilongjiang Province trained as many as 1,359 middle and high school students for vocational skills for up to two years (Xinjiang Yearook 2013, 115). Furthermore, another common practice is to select local middle school graduates to attend high schools at the assistance providing regions. Jiangxi Province, the assistance partner with Kizilsu Kyrgiz Autonomous Prefecture, has been enrolling 100 middle school graduates to attend a high school in Nanchang, the capital city of Jiangxi on an annual basis (Xinjiang Yearbook, 2013, 129). Many provinces and municipalities in the coastal and central regions have opened "*Xinjiang neigaoban*" (inland high school classes for Xinjiang students).

Furthermore, tremendous resources have also been devoted to the construction and enhancement of education infrastructures such as educational centers and bilingual schools. What seems to be the focus of attention is the creation of a large number of bilingual kindergartens across the region. Indeed, the rapid growth of bilingual kindergartens throughout Xinjiang in recent years is a strong indicator that the Chinese government is addressing the problem of racial tension by instigating changes in important social institutions. Children of ethnic minority background from a very young age are socialized into developing identities that emphasize being a citizen of the integrated nation of the PRC.

Relative to northern Xinjiang, there is a higher level of commitment to both educational assistance in general and bilingual education in particular in southern Xinjiang. The reason for this is clear. Southern Xinjiang is known for being the breeding ground for anti-PRC sentiment (Mackerras 2001) and the enhancement of education is expected to help reduce the racial tension. In the three districts of Kashgar, Hotan and Kizilsu, for example, nearly half

(47 percent) of all assistance-affiliated projects and two-thirds (67 percent) of all assistance funding were devoted to education assistance in 2013. The following five provinces or municipalities ranked at the top with total financial commitment to education in 2013: Jiangsu (assisting Kizilsu and Yili), Beijing (assisting Hotan), Zhejiang (assisting Aksu), Shanghai (assisting Kashgar) and Shandong (assisting Kashgar) (Xinjiang Yearbook 2014, 110). As an illustrative case, the following section is an in-depth analysis of the educational assistance program in Hotan in southern Xinjiang.

With a population that is nearly exclusively Uyghur (98 percent), Hotan receives assistance from three administrative units: Beijing and Tianjin municipalities and Anhui Province. All of them have made bilingual education the utmost priority in their assistance programs. Beijing is assigned to provide aid to the city of Hotan and the three counties of Hotan, Moyu and Luopu. With the resources provided by Beijing, as many as six bilingual educational facilities were built and 1,440 bilingual teachers were trained during the year of 2011. In following years of 2012, 2013 and 2014, at least 1,060, 500 and 1,600 additional teachers were trained respectively with Beijing's assistance. In other words, based on reports in Xinjiang yearbooks, at least 4,600 teachers received bilingual training via Beijing's assistance program for the three counties and the city of Hotan between 2011 and 2014. While many teachers are trained locally, 90 so-called "backbone" bilingual teachers were selected to receive more intensive training at Beijing Normal University in 2013 and this figure rose to 120 in 2014 (Xinjiang Yearbook 2013, 111; 2014, 133). There is little doubt that these 90 teachers were recruited through a highly selective process and, upon completion of the training, they would be expected to play a significant role in Xinjiang's bilingual education as well as the overall development of Xinjiang.

Tianjin, which is matched with the three counties of Cele, Yutian and Minfeng in Hotan District, provided bilingual training to at least 2,051 teachers from 2012 to 2014. In addition, Tianjin arranged to have scores of teachers as well as administrative and professional personnel to receive training in Tianjin in both 2012 and 2013 (Xinjiang Yearbooks 2012–2015).

Anhui Province, which was assigned to assist the county of Pishan in Hotan, trained 550 bilingual teachers in 2012. The following year, in 2013, 100 teachers received full-time bilingual training for a whole year. Anhui also helped build, among other educational facilities, as many as 30 bilingual kindergartens in Pishan County (Xinjiang Yearbook 2012, 157). Staffed with mostly newly trained teachers, all the 30 bilingual kindergartens started recruiting students since 2011 (Yearbook 2012, 157). In sum, the three provinces and cities of Beijing, Tianjin and Anhui helped train at least more than 7,000 bilingual teachers for Hotan District between 2011 and 2014.

In addition to standard measures of training bilingual teachers, many cities and provinces have tried alternative approaches in order to discover talents and explore resources in the search for qualified teachers and address the problem of the severe teacher shortage in bilingual education. It is reported, for instance, that 70 individuals who originally were not officially certified as teachers (*fei zhengshi jiaoshi*) received bilingual training of pre-school education, which was offered by educational assistance of Beijing in 2011. Fifty-three of them passed the provincial-level exam after they had completed the training (Xinjiang Yearbook 2012, 153). Anhui allocates one million yuan annually that is earmarked as financial reward to teachers in Pishan County who have reached the required standard of Mandarin language proficiency level through independent learning (Xinjiang Yearbook 2012, 157). In addition, a variety of other programs and activities have been arranged to promote bilingual education, such as the annual "competition in bilingual education." These competitions and events often involve as many as thousands of participants each time.

ASSISTANCE PROGRAM AND XINJIANG'S HIGHER EDUCATIONAL INSTITUTIONS

When China was under a planned economy, higher education was, just like all other social institutions and organizations, strictly controlled by the state. It was in response to the state's calls and assignment that higher educational institutions engaged in and disseminated research. This situation has changed since the reform. Increasingly, higher educational institutions, especially prestigious ones, are expected to assist with designing policies and solving problems in economic development, environmental degradation, cultural and racial confrontations and any other areas that are deemed as in need of advice from academic and scholarly talent and think tanks (Rhoads, et al. 2014). The input and contributions of higher educational institutions in the economic and technological development, in particular, are considered essential in realizing China's ambitious plans for economic development. "Knowledge economy," a concept that was non-existent in pre-reform China, has developed rapidly whereby institutions create and develop knowledge and technology and transfer them to the economic field. Even though most of the technology transfers are exercised by prestigious institutions such as Qinghua, which is often referred to as "China's MIT," other institutions are expected to catch up with this trend as well (Yang and Welch 2012).

Following this pattern, Xinjiang University, the most prestigious institution and one of two institutions in the region that are participants in Project

211,[5] has been receiving a tremendous amount of attention in the assistance program whereby a team of ten institutions, with Qinghua University as the leader, have been assigned to assist Xinjiang University. The expected results of the assistance and nurturing are clear: so Xinjiang University, just like its most significant mentoring institution, Qinghua, would produce talent, knowledge and technology, all of which would then be transferred to fostering economic and social development plans in Xinjiang.

Assistance to higher education in Xinjiang was officially placed on the agenda of the assistance program as early as 2005. Initially, as is shown in Table 6.1, as many as 40 higher educational institutions from inland and coastal areas were called upon to help train scientists and academic personnel, provide information, technology and facilities, and develop and improve corresponding academic programs (Baike 2010; 2016). In other words, this assistance program of higher education initially had a very academic-oriented goal and was designed primarily to help enhance the quality of Xinjiang's higher education. According to the layout of the program, each of the scores of institutions are required to provide assistance in approximately three academic discipline areas. The recipients of the assistance included 11 of Xinjiang's colleges and universities, which was an exhaustive list of all higher educational institutions in Xinjiang at that time.[6]

The assistance program to Xinjiang's higher education experienced significant changes in the most recent revision of the program in 2010. First of all, there was a major shift of participants in both the assistance providing institutions as well as recipient institutions in Xinjiang in the program. The outcome of the shift is that there was a heavy emphasis on applied science and technology. Nearly all comprehensive universities as well as institutions that were not STEM-oriented were dropped from the list of institutions that had provided assistance to Xinjiang's higher education. Furthermore, all participating institutions, according to the 2010 revision, are among the most prestigious higher educational institutions in China. All of them are participants in Project 211 and the majority of them are participants in Project 985 as well, as is show in Table 6.2 (see Note v).

Furthermore, there were dramatic differences at the receiving end as a result of changes that took place in the program in 2010. Only three institutions were designated as participants in Xinjiang: Xinjiang University, Shihezi University, and Tarim University.[7] While Xinjiang University receives assistance from a group of institutions with Qinghua University as the leader, Shihezi University is mentored by institutions headed by Beijing University (which is dubbed "China's Harvard") and Tarim University is matched with China Agricultural University and a few other institutions (see Table 6.2).

Table 6.1 The 2005 Model of Higher Educational Assistance Program in Xinjiang: Institutions and Academic Areas

Institutions in Xinjiang	
Institutions providing the assistance	Academic disciplines in which assistance was provided
Xinjiang University	
Beijing University	Chemistry, biology
Qinghua University	Electric engineering, computer science and technology
Wuhan University	Mathematics, mapping science and technology, law
Xi'an Jiaotong University	Mechanical engineering, business management & engineering, control science & technology
Dalian University of Science and Technology	Chemical engineering and technology
Beijing Jiaotong University	Traffic and transportation engineering, business management and engineering
Tarim University	
Donghua University	Textile science and technology
Tongji University	Civil engineering, architecture
Shanghai Jiaotong University	Physics, information and communication engineering
Beijing Foreign Languages University	Foreign languages and literature
China University of Mining and Technology	Geological resources and engineering, mining engineering
Zhejiang University	Animal husbandry, economic management of agriculture and forestry, biology
Sichuan Agriculture University	Cropology
Northwestern Agriculture and Forestry University	Horticulture, veterinary science, vegetation protection
China Agricultural University	Agricultural engineering, utilization of agricultural resources, veterinary science, biology
Beijing Forestry University	Forestry science
Northeastern Agricultural University	Agricultural engineering, animal husbandry, veterinary science
Xinjiang Agriculture University	
Nanjing Agricultural University	Cropology, economic management of agriculture and forestry, veterinary science
Hehai University	Water conservancy engineering
Shihezi University	
Tianjin University	Chemical engineering and technology
Huazhong University of Science and Technology	Basic medicine, internal medicine, public health, and preventive medicine
Jiangnan University	Food science and engineering

Table 6.1 Continued

Xinjiang Medical University	
Zhongshan University	Basic medicine, ophthalmology, oncology
Zhongnan University	Internal medicine
China Medical University	Pharmacy
Fudan University	Surgery, public, and preventive medicine
Beijing Chinese Medical University	Combination of Chinese and western medicine, Chinese medicine
Xinjiang Normal University	
Beijing Normal University	Psychology, education
Huadong Normal University	Geography, Chinese language and literature, physical education
China University of Science and Technology	Chemistry, mathematics, and physics
Xinjiang Finance Institute	
China People's University	Applied economics, news and mass media, law
Central University of Finance & Economics	Applied economics, business management
Xinjiang Art Institute	
Chinese University of Mass Media	Chinese language, literature, and art
Chinese Music Academy	Art
Kashgar Normal College	
Huanan Normal University	Education
Nankai University	Physics, mathematics, chemistry
Yili Normal College	
Northeastern Normal University	Education, biology
Nanjing University	Physics, chemistry, mathematics
Changji College	
Jilin University	Chemistry, foreign languages and literature
Shandong University	Mathematics, physics

Source: Guoqing.china.com.cn 2011.

SUMMARY

Educational assistance to Xinjiang focuses on bilingual education that is operationalized as the elimination, albeit gradually, of ethnic minority languages and the exclusive use of Mandarin in the region's educational system. To replace the Uyghur language with the Mandarin as the only educational medium in Xinjiang, however, is by no means easy given the large size and heavy concentration of Uyghur population and the strong sense of Uyghur

Table 6.2 Participating Universities and Their Status in the 2010 Assistance Program in Xinjiang

Institution	*Status*
XINJIANG UNIVERSITY	
Qinghua University*	211, 985
Xian Jiaotong University^	211, 985
Wuhan University^	211, 985
Zhongnan University^	211, 985
Beijing Normal University	211, 985
Beijing Foreign Languages University	211
Dalian University of Technology	211, 985
Tongji University	211, 985
Donghua University	211
China University of Mining and Technology	211
SHIHEZI UNIVERSITY	
Beijing University*	211, 985
Huazhong University of Science and Technology^	211, 985
East China University of Science and Technology^	211, 985
Huazhong Agricultural University	211
Chongqing University	211, 985
Jiangnan University	211
University of International Business and Economics	211
Nanjing Normal University	211
South China Agricultural University	211
TARIM UNIVERSITY	
China Agricultural University*	211, 985
Zhejiang University^	211, 985
Huazhong Agricultural University^	211
Beijing University of Chemical Technology	211, 985
Donghua University	211

*Designated team leader.
^Designated associate team leader.

ethnic identity, especially in southern Xinjiang. An enormous amount of resources of the assistance program have been devoted to this transformation with the majority of the funding on training of bilingual teachers and the construction of bilingual facilities.

Language policies in Xinjiang help facilitate the CCP's long-term goal of modernizing the country and raising its power and influence in the world. Based on the discussion in this chapter, ethnic minority languages and culture are considered inadequate or even obstructive by the authority in the national-building process. Institutionalized efforts to marginalize the language, culture, and identity of ethnic minority populations, however, may aggravate the already tense ethnic relations in the region. The situation may become even more serious with the growth of discrepancy of overall well-being and quality of life between the Han and minority populations in Xinjiang, as will be discussed in the next chapter.

NOTES

1. Incidentally, the secessionist Eastern Turkistan Republic (ETR) that succeeded Sheng's regime also valued education and contributed significantly to further development of education in the territories controlled by this rebellious government (Benson 2004, 193–194).

2. In her research, Tsung presents quotes by a Uyghur interviewee, who is a teacher at a school in southern Xinjiang. "If you want to live in our region, Uyghur should be learnt and taught to Han students in schools. The majority of people here are Uyghurs. Of course we need to learn the Han language. Everyone knows it is important to learn the Han language, but our Uyghur language is also important" (Tsung 2014, 174). It should be noted that the interviewee who made these remarks teaches at a county school. The negative sentiment and resentment are very likely even stronger in rural schools in southern Xinjiang where the population is nearly exclusively Uyghur.

3. Not only is it difficult to find and maintain qualified teachers, but there is another problem. Not all existing bilingual teachers are qualified or effective in their teaching. Partly to solve this problem and partly to meet the expectation since the reform that professionals be evaluated with objective standards, increasingly rigorous evaluation schemes have been developed to ensure quality control of teaching Mandarin language to minority students. The Chinese language proficiency test, or HSK (*hanyu shuiping kaoshi*), designed in 1990, is probably the most frequently used tool in assessing minority language teachers' job performance. Teachers who have not met the standard are expected to either retire or face the danger of losing their jobs (Dwyer 2004, 33&40; Yaynen 2006; Schluessel 2007, 257).

4. The average urban residents in Xinjiang earned 19,874 yuan in 2013. (*Xinjiang Statistical Yearbook* 2015, 22–23).

5. Projects 211 and 985 were programs designed and implemented by the Chinese government during the 1990s to strengthen the quality of research and management of major universities in China. The enrollment and participation in these programs have been frequently used as key indicators to identify and recognize the ranking of the status of top universities in China (Rhoads, et al. 2014). There are 116 institutions in China that are selected to participate in Project 211, which makes up about 6 percent of all higher educational institutions in China. Participation in Project 985 is even more competitive and deemed more prestigious, since the membership has been granted to only 39 institutions. In addition to prestige and status recognition, there are financial incentives for becoming members of these projects. Once admitted, all participants are entitled to a tremendous amount of funding and resources awarded by the government. Besides, the funding that the participating institutions are entitled

to is hierarchically distributed. For example, while most of the participating universities in the 985 project received hundreds of millions of yuan as funding resources, Qinghua University and Beijing University each received 1.8 billion yuan for being enrolled in this project.

6. These institutions include Xinjiang University, Tarim University, Shehezi University, Xinjiang Agricultural University, Xinjiang Medical University, Xinjiang Normal University, Xinjiang Institute of Finance and Economics, Xinjiang Institute of Art, Kashgar Normal Institute, Yli Normal Institute and Changji Institute.

7. There is a tendency in recent years to include educational institutions in addition to the three listed in this table as recipients of help from the assistance program, according to Xinjiang Yearbooks.

Chapter 7

Assistance in Health Care and Welfare Programs in Xinjiang

One of the most controversial issues concerning PRC's policies in regard to Xinjiang's development is the imbalanced nature between stimulating the economic development on the one hand and enhancing the quality of life and well-being of local populations on the other. Studies have repeatedly shown that overwhelming emphasis has been placed on Xinjiang's expected role of supplier of material resources for China's industrial development, most of which takes place in the coastal region, while the well-being of local region has not received nearly as much attention. This helps explain the fact that Xinjiang has seen a tremendous amount of construction and development of its infrastructure and projects for the extraction, processing, and transportation of natural resources. Furthermore, Xinjiang's economy has been over-represented by heavy industry and state-owned enterprises (Becquelin 2000, 2004; Chaudhuri 2005). At the same time, the overall quality of life of Xinjiang's population is far below the national average. With the GDP growth at a rate of 10.3 percent from 1978 to 2000 (Chaudhuri 2005) and a level comparable with that of China as a whole since then (Szadziewski 2011; see also Table 7.1), Xinjiang's economy is among the most advanced within the western region of China. However, the quality of life and overall well-being of Xinjiang's population do not seem to match the ranking of its economic development level, as is shown in the disposable income distribution and health status of the population in Xinjiang (see Table 7.1).

Table 7.1 Average GDP (Yuan) and Disposable Income (Yuan) in Xinjiang and China, 1980–2015

	Xinjiang (yuan)				*China (yuan)*			
	Urban Income	*Rural Income*	*Ratio Ur/Ru*	*GDP/capita*	*Urban Income*	*Rural Income*	*Ratio Ur/Ru*	*GDP/capita*
1980	553	200	2.76	410	477	191	2.47	464
1985	797	394	2.02	820	739	397	1.86	860
1990	1,432	683	2.09	1,713	1,510	686	2.20	1,654
1995	4,183	1,136	3.68	4,701	4,283	1,577	2.71	5,074
2000	5,686	1,618	3.51	7,372	6,280	2,254	2.78	7,902
2005	7,990	2,482	3.22	13,108	10,493	3,254	3.22	14,259
2006	8,871	2,737	3.24	15,000	11,759	3,587	3.27	16,602
2007	10,313	3,183	3.24	16,999	13,785	4,140	3.32	20,337
2008	11,432	3,502	3.26	19,893	15,780	4,760	3.31	23,912
2009	12,257	3,883	3.15	19,942	17,174	5,153	3.33	25,963
2010	13,643	4,642	2.93	25,034	19,109	5,919	3.22	30,567
2011	15,513	5,442	2.85	30,087	21,809	6,977	3.12	36,018
2012	17,920	6,393	2.80	33,796	24,564	7,916	3.10	39,544
2013	21,091	7,846	2.68	37,553	26,467	9,429	2.80	43,220
2014	23,214	8,723	2.66	40,648	28,844	10,488	2.75	46,629
2015	26,275	9,425	2.78	40,036	31,194	11,421	2.73	49,351

Source: *Xinjiang and China Statistics Yearbooks*.

ECONOMIC DEVELOPMENT AND URBAN VS. RURAL INCOME DISTRIBUTIONS IN XINJIANG AND CHINA

Table 7.1 lists the average GDP as well as urban and rural average incomes of residents in Xinjiang and in China as a whole since 1980. According to the table, Xinjiang's economic development (measured in terms of GDP per capita) and material quality of life and well-being (measured in terms of the average income of residents) both, in general, lag behind the average values for China as a whole. But the extent of the difference in disposable income is greater compared with that of the economic development, indicating that Xinjiang is ranked lower in overall quality of life compared with the economic well-being. Let us use the year 2008 as an example. Whereas the average GDP per capita in China as a whole was 20 percent higher compared with that of Xinjiang in 2008, the average income in urban and rural areas in China was, respectively, 38 percent and 36 percent higher than the average income of urban and rural residents in Xinjiang. This pattern has been persistent since the 1990s. The implementation of the most recent assistance program has not really changed the situation significantly even though people's livelihood and quality of life are said to have received more attention compared with the economic development in the program. These results confirm research findings concerning China's policy on Xinjiang that devotes more emphasis on the economic development of the region than the quality of life of residents (Becquelin 2000, 2004; Chaudhuri 2005).

Another pattern that can be observed from Table 7.1 is that, consistent with the tendency in China as a whole, urban residents have been earning a significantly higher income compared with their rural counterparts in Xinjiang and this gap kept increasing until recent years. In 1980, the ratio between urban and rural average income in Xinjiang was 2.76, which decreased to 2.02 by the mid-1980s when urban residents earned roughly twice as much as rural residents. By the mid-1990s, however, the ratio between urban and rural average income rose dramatically to as high as 3.68, suggesting that urban residents, on average, earned close to four times as much income as rural residents toward the end of the 1990s. Even though the gap narrowed somewhat during the following years, the ratio of urban-rural income fluctuated from around 3.2 to 3.6 throughout the 2000s. It was only after 2010, which was when the most recent version of the assistance program was implemented, that the gap gradually narrowed. By 2014, the urban-rural income difference, with a ratio of 2.66, became similar to that at the beginning of the reform nearly four decades earlier.

The urban versus rural income difference in Xinjiang has profound and multifaceted implications. First of all, as the data in Table 7.2 show, Xinjiang has been a rural region despite the gradual increase of its urbanization level

Table 7.2 Percent of Urban Population in Xinjiang, 1949–2014

1949	*1955*	*1960*	*1965*	*1970*	*1975*	*1980*	*1985*	*1990*	*2000*	*2005*	*2010*	*2014*	*2015*
12.2	15.1	26.2	18.6	17.7	22.5	29.0	42.7	44.8	33.7	37.1	42.8	46.1	47.2

since the founding of the PRC. When the reform first started in 1980, only 29 percent of Xinjiang's population lived in urban areas. The proportion of urban population has changed drastically since then, but it has never reached 50 percent. Currently, 54 percent of Xinjiang's population still resides in nonurban areas who, as the above discussion indicates, earn significantly less income than their urban counterparts.

Second, the differentiation of urban versus rural income distribution is highly correlated with other factors as well, such as regional and geographic variations and the composition of ethnic populations in communities in Xinjiang. Southern Xinjiang, where the vast majority of the population is Uyghur, suffers from an extremely low level of economic development. All southern districts (Hotan, Kashgar, Kizilsu, and Aksu) are at the bottom of Xinjiang's prefecture-level units that are ranked according to the GDP per capita, as was discussed in chapters 1 and 5. Besides, the urbanization level in southern Xinjiang is significantly lower compared with the rest of Xinjiang. In Kashgar and Hotan, only about one-third of the population live in urban areas.

POVERTY AND RACIAL STRATIFICATION IN XINJIANG

The destitute condition of southern Xinjiang's extremely poor quality of life and its relationship with ethnic compositions and urbanization level can be assessed through results generated by China's poverty combat programs.

China has launched a series of campaigns to combat poverty, which is referred to as the "*fupin* (扶贫)" (poverty-alleviation) program. With numerous revisions since its conception during the 1980s, the *fupin* program has reflected China's rapidly changing economic and social conditions over the decades (Cheng 2011; Fan et al. 2016). For example, the program in recent years no longer has any coverage in the coastal region. All the 592 counties currently enrolled in the program are located in either the western or the central region of China.[1] Poverty counties are identified based on multiple indicators such as GDP per capita and average income of residents. Once designated as being poverty-stricken and enrolled in the program, these counties are eligible to receive funds and financial support from the government (Fan et al. 2016).

Affirmative action and other preferential policies have been implemented to accommodate counties with "special characteristics" to qualify for government funding under the *fupin* program. One of the most frequently cited criteria is the extent to which the communities are predominantly inhabited by ethnic minority populations.[2] Threshold standard was altered so it is relatively easier for these areas and administrative units to be designated as poverty-stricken.

China Statistics Press publishes a data source titled Xinjiang Survey Yearbook. The data source devotes one section to Xinjiang's *fupin* program. According to the 2010 edition of the data source, among all the 68 counties in Xinjiang, 27 were officially identified as being poverty-stricken.[3] The vast majority of them (21counties or 77 percent of poverty-stricken counties in Xinjiang) were located in southern Xinjiang with eight in Kashgar, seven in Hotan, four in Kizilsu, and two in Aksu (Cheng 2011). The heavy concentration of poverty-stricken counties in southern Xinjiang is probably the major reason that information on poverty in Xinjiang are organized in two separate datasets in the Survey Yearbook. One dataset provides information for poverty villages in the 27 poverty-stricken counties in Xinjiang as a whole and the other one is for poverty-stricken villages of the three districts of Kashgar, Hotan, and Kizilsu in southern Xinjiang. The last two rows in Table 7.3 show, respectively, the information for all poverty-stricken villages in Xinjiang as a whole and those in the three districts in southern Xinjiang.[4]

According to Table 7.3, there were a total of 181 poverty villages in the whole region of Xinjiang. Seventy-six percent (*N*=138) of them were located in the three southern districts mentioned above. The proportion of ethnic minority populations in all poverty-stricken villages in Xinjiang was 93.3 percent, whereas this figure was 99.6 percent in the 138 poverty-stricken villages in the three southern districts. In other words, while the vast majority of the population in poverty-stricken villages in Xinjiang were ethnic minorities, the populations in poverty-stricken counties in southern Xinjiang are virtually all ethnic minorities, Uyghurs specifically.

Table 7.3 also lists the average income of the eight prefecture-level units and of Xinjiang in general. The rural average income in the districts of Kashgar (2,983 yuan) and Hotan (2,318 yuan) was significantly lower than Xinjiang's average rural income of 3,883 yuan. The rural income in districts in northern Xinjiang, on the other hand, was all significantly above the rural average income in the region. In addition, according to Table 7.3, the average income of all poverty villages in Xinjiang was 2,810 yuan, which was 27 percent less than the average rural income in Xinjiang as a whole. The average income of the 138 poverty-stricken villages in the three southern districts (2,502 yuan), on the other hand, was more than a third (38 percent) less than what the average farmer in Xinjiang earned in 2009. Table 7.3

Table 7.3 Rural Average Income of Selected Districts and Poverty Villages in Xinjiang and Southern Xinjiang, 2009

Units	*Ave. Income** *Yuan*	*Population*	*Pct Minority Population^* *%*	*Urbanization Level 2014^* *%*
Xinjiang	3,883		60	46
Changji (north)	6,572		27	85
Yili (north)	4,510		58	59
Tacheng (north)	4,984		28	79
Altay (north)	4,340		59	56
Bayingol (north)	6,784		44	79
Aksu (south)	4,531		81	64
Kashgar (south)	2,983		93	37
Hotan (south)	2,318		96	35
Poverty Villages, Xinjiang (*N*=181)	2,810		93.3*	N/A
Poverty Villages, southern Xinjiang (*N*=138)	2,502		99.6*	N/A

Xinjiang Survey Yearbook 2010, Table 2–28 and Table 4–6;
^*Xinjiang Statistics Yearbook* 2015.

further demonstrates the truly destitute situation that rural areas in Hotan suffer from. With an average income of 2,318 yuan in 2009, an average farmer in Hotan earned less than the average income of farmers in poverty counties in southern Xinjiang, which was 2,502 yuan, in 2009.

The destitute economic conditions in Xinjiang, especially southern Xinjiang, are probably major factors that help explain the poor health and quality of life in Xinjiang, which are deemed far more important by researchers in the assessment of overall well-being of communities and populations. As Nobel Laureate Amartya Sen points out, to improve economic welfare, attention should not be focused on economic conditions only. Instead, it should emphasize people's capabilities to transform economic resources to nontangible elements such as freedom of living a healthy life and pursuing activities and goals that they personally value. Sen argues specifically that the capability of living a healthy and long life should be one of the most important components of the assessment of people's happiness and well-being (Sen 1985).

HEALTH OF XINJIANG'S POPULATION

According to health statistics, Xinjiang ranks at the bottom among China's provinces according to health status of its population. This is consistently the case when health is measured in terms of multiple indicators such as infant mortality rate (IMR), maternal mortality rate (MMR), or life expectancy, and this pattern has persisted since at least the early 1980s when provincial-level health statistics in China started to be made available.

In 1981, Xinjiang's IMR was 115, which was the highest in the nation, albeit the IMR data for Tibet were not available in the data source. It was more than three times as high as the national average, which was 37.7 at the time. By 1990, Xinjiang's IMR dropped to 58.5, but was still among the highest in the country and more than twice as high as the national average of 27.3 (China Health Statistics 2007, Table 8-2-3). IMR in Xinjiang dropped significantly to 14.27 in 2014, the most recent data available when this manuscript was written. But compared with the figure for the country (5.37), it is still very high (Almanac of Chinas Population 2015, Table 91)).

MMR is measured as the number of maternal deaths among every 10,000 pregnant women as a result of complications associated with pregnancy or childbirth. In 2006, Xinjiang's MMR was 92.1, which was nearly three times as high as that for China as a whole (which was 34.8). Only Tibet, with the MMR of 244.1, ranked higher than Xinjiang on this measure among all provincial-level administrative units in China for that year (China Health Statistics 2007, Table 7-2-2). The MMR in Xinjiang reduced to 39.1 in 2014, which was still more than five times as high as the national average figure (7.7) and was the second highest in the country (next to Tibet) (Almanac of China's Population 2015, Table 95).

Xinjiang's life expectancy has improved significantly considering it was only around 30 at the time of the founding of the PRC (Dautcher 2004). But it is still among the lowest in China. The national average life expectancy in China was 68.55 and 71.4 in 1990 and 2000, respectively, whereas Xinjiang's life expectancy was 63.59 and 67.41, respectively, for these two-year periods. Only three or four other provinces or autonomous regions, all of them located in western China, had lower life expectancies compared with Xinjiang in China during these years (China Health Statistics 2007, Table 8-2-3).

These quality-of-life measures beg for explanations for the relatively poor health of Xinjiang's population. Unfortunately, there are few systematic studies that examine health in Xinjiang. Besides, health-related studies on the population in China as a whole tend to marginalize or even exclude frontier regions, such as Xinjiang and Tibet, in their research (e.g., Anson and Sun 2005; Bloom and Tang 2004), citing reasons such as complications and difficulties in gathering accurate information in these areas (Zeng et al. 2008). Not surprisingly, therefore, limited research on health in Xinjiang has sometimes shown inconsistent results, making it even more difficult to reach generalizations and conclusions. For example, ecological and environmental problems, such as air, soil, and water pollutions, have been cited by researchers as major contributing factors that damage public health in Xinjiang

(Ingram 2001; Scull 2011). One other research report, based on data during the similar time period, has suggested that health risk in Xinjiang, due to composite factors such as air and water pollution, poor nutrition, and inadequate access to health services, is among the lowest in the nation (WHO and UNDP 2001).

What does seem to have been repeatedly and consistently demonstrated in research studies is that there are tremendous health variations within Xinjiang due to demographic and socioeconomic characteristics. The most important health predictor seems to be race and ethnic composition. The Han population enjoys better health compared with ethnic minorities such as the Uyghur. Studies have shown, for example, that there is a difference in terms of tooth decay and fluoride ingestion between the Uyghur and Han children who live in the same communities and attend the same schools, "Uyghur children ingested more fluoride and had more tooth decay than their Han classmates" (Schuster 2009, 439). Research also shows that the concentration of the Han population is a significantly positive factor and that of the Uyghur population a significantly negative factor in the explanation of health of elderly population in counties and cities in Xinjiang (Li and Dorsten 2011). The difference between Han and Uyghur health persists when health is measured in terms of both objective assessment, such as IMR (Schuster 2009) and MMR (Du et al. 2009), as well as subjective self-evaluations (Li and Dorsten 2011). And the same pattern holds in studies that are based on secondary data analysis of aggregate information (Li and Dorsten 2011; Schuster 2009) as well as research that analyzes survey results of individual data (Du et al. 2009; Feng et al. 2014).

The Han population enjoys better health compared with not just the Uyghur, but all other ethnic groups such as the Mongol, the Kyrgiz, and the Tajik. Table 7.4 presents descriptive statistics of average IMRs of

Table 7.4 Descriptive Statistics for IMR in Districts and Townships Predominantly Inhabited by Various Ethnic Groups and by Mixed Racial Groups in Xinjiang, 2000

	Mean	*Stand Deviation*	*Minimum*	*Maximum*	N
Han	11.59	16.52	0	125	510
Hui	17.25	9.62	6.21	38.5	14
Mixed Race	19.84	26.59	0	144.74	121
Kazak	28.38	40.6	0	333.33	153
Tajik	33.99	38.2	0	111.11	13
Uyghur	43.44	36.22	0	228.57	465
Kirgiz	48.37	52.9	0	187.5	29
Mongol	71.15	94.85	0	307.6	15
Provincial	27.38	34.86	0	333.33	1320

Source: China County/District Population Census Data Assemblies 2000.

communities predominantly inhabited by major ethnic populations at the rural township and city district level in Xinjiang in 2000. Compared with provincial- or county-level health data, township and district data are measured at more of a disaggregate level. The 96 county-level administrative units in Xinjiang, for example, contain 1,320 rural townships or urban districts. Consequently, compared with aggregate data at county or city level, data at the level of townships and districts are likely to provide more valid information since, among other things, they help reduce or avoid the problem of ecological fallacy (Puntscher et al. 2016).

In Table 7.4, the 1,320 rural townships or urban districts are organized according to the predominance of one or multiple ethnic groups, which is defined as a minimum of 50 percent of the residency. For example, there are 510 townships and districts where at least 50 percent of the residents are Han and there are 465 communities that are predominantly inhabited by the Uyghur. A little less than 10 percent (*N*=121) of the townships and districts do not have any particular ethnic group that make up the demographic majority of the residents, hence they are labeled as mixed-race communities.[5]

According to Table 7.4, rural townships and city districts with the Han, the Hui, or mixed ethnic groups as dominant residents have the highest health status with the lowest average IMR values. On the other hand, communities predominantly inhabited by the Mongol, the Kyrgiz, the Uyghur, and the Tajik have significantly lower health status, as is shown with their relatively high average IMRs. The average IMRs of Uyghur- and Kyrgiz-dominant communities are about four times as high as that of Han-dominant communities. The difference of average IMRs between Mongol and Han communities is even more astounding, with the former being six-plus times greater than the latter.

Not only are Han, Hui, and mixed-race communities relatively healthier, but there is a smaller degree of variations in terms of IMRs in these communities. In other words, rural townships and urban districts with the Han, the Hui, and mixed-race as dominant residents tend to be similar to one another in the sense that relatively few infants die in them. Communities with poor health, inhabited predominantly by Kazak, Mongol, and Uyghur, on the other hand, tend to be different from one another in this regard: while some experience no infant deaths, others would encounter infant deaths as high as around one-third of all new born children before they reach their first birthday.

In addition to the racial composition, poor health is likely a result of other factors as well. Educational achievement has been found to be a significant factor in health variation and in the acquisition of health-related knowledge in Xinjiang (Schuster 2009; Yuan et al. 2015). Furthermore, there is a health divide between urban and rural areas. Compared with urban residents, rural populations, particularly rural Uyghur population, are more likely to develop noncommunicable diseases (Feng et al. 2014). In addition, research has shown that in western China, including Xinjiang, average income per capita in both cities and rural areas has a positive impact on health (Du et al. 2009). Low income and economic hardship were found to be the most important reason for residents in poverty-stricken areas in Xinjiang to not pursue medical help when they are ill, according to the survey mentioned above (Xinjiang Survey Yearbook 2010 Table 4–5). Besides, this relationship becomes stronger with the increase of poverty level. According to the survey yearbook, as high a proportion as 91.8 percent of residents of poverty-stricken villages in Xinjiang stated economic hardship being the reason they would not visit doctors when ill, but this figure jumped to 95.6 percent for poverty-stricken villages in southern Xinjiang (Survey Yearbook 2010, Table 4–5).

The conference on the assistance program in Xinjiang and the Beijing conference on Xinjiang, both held in 2010, apparently took into consideration the overall poor quality of material life and particularly the low-level well-being of rural areas and ethnic minority populations in Xinjiang. Decisions were made at both conferences that "the improvement of people's wellbeing is to receive utmost priorities in the program (民生优先)" (Xinjiang Yearbook 2011, 38 and 45; People. Cn 2014).

ASSISTANCE PROGRAM TO ENHANCE THE WELL-BEING OF XINJIANG'S POPULATION SINCE 2010

Dual-dwelling project:

Among the numerous programs to improve the quality of life of residents in Xinjiang, the "dual-dwelling projects" (两居工程), referred to, respectively, as 安居富民 (*anju fumin*) and 安居兴牧 (*anju xingmu*), seem to have received the most attention, based on the fact that they are the first items to be addressed in official documents and reports on the assistance program, such as Xinjiang yearbooks. "*Anju fumin*" means to provide comfortable living facilities to farmers so to help them become prosperous, whereas "*anju xingmu*" means to provide herdsmen dwelling facilities to live a settled life in order to help invigorate animal husbandry production. The core of the dual-dwelling programs, consequently, is the renovation and construction of residential dwelling facilities for both farmers and herdsmen in Xinjiang.

One of the most urgent tasks in achieving the above goal was to repair the large number of houses throughout Xinjiang that were in a hazardous condition because they had been damaged by natural disasters such as earthquakes and storms over the years. The first year or so of the recent wave of the assistance program saw many of these houses being repaired, renovated, or rebuilt.

For example, in 2010, Liaoning Province, which is assigned to assist Tacheng District in northern Xinjiang, rebuilt more than seven thousand houses that were deemed unsafe in one village alone of Yumin County (Xinjiang Yearbook 2011, 44).

Meanwhile, all provinces and cities involved in the assistance program have been vigorously engaged in large-scale projects to construct or renovate houses for farmers and nomadic populations in Xinjiang. According to the Xinjiang Yearbook, in 2012, 3.89 billion yuan, which made up 34.1 percent of the total amount of assistance fund by the 19 assistance-providing units for that year, was devoted to the dual-dwelling projects (Xinjiang Yearbook 2013, 119). During the following two years, 2013 and 2014, an additional 3.43 and 3.91 billion yuan respectively were committed to this project (Xinjiang Yearbook 2014, 109, 2015, 130). As a result, hundreds of thousands of houses have been built each year throughout Xinjiang, mostly in rural and pastoral areas.

Let us use Beijing that is matched with the city of Hotan and three counties in Hotan District in southern Xinjiang as an example to illustrate the fast pace and large volume of housing construction. During the four years from 2011 to 2014, Beijing built, respectively, 32,615, 24,000, 28,500, and 31,605 houses, with the combined total number of 116,720, in Hotan. If we assume that on average four people live in each household, this means close to half a million people in Hotan have lived in houses that are either newly built or upgraded since the most recent wave of the assistance program. Hunan Province that is assigned to assist Turpan is another case in point. It constructed 1,000 houses in 2010 and this figure increased significantly during the following years with 6,160 in 2011, 8,640 in 2012 and 11,000 in 2013 (All figures in this paragraph are based on Xinjiang Yearbooks of relevant years).

During my visit to southern Xinjiang in 2013, I was struck by the rows of newly built homes in rural areas of Hotan. Surrounded by fruit trees and farmlands, the houses have front and back yards as well as convenient and nicely, and newly, paved roads. According to the yearbooks and individuals who showed a group of us around, detailed thoughts and planning were devoted to the design of the interior of the houses as well. Practical and functional facilities and devices such as running water, electricity, gas, kitchen, bathrooms, and shower have been made available in these houses. Shanghai, for example, spent 337 million yuan to construct 30,280 houses for farmers and 745 houses for herdsmen in Kashgar region in 2014 with an additional 146 million yuan on infrastructures associated with these houses such as running water, electricity, road construction, and so on (Xinjiang Yearbook 2015, 134). For many local residents, this is probably the first time some of these appliances, devices, and infrastructure have been introduced to their dwelling units, which has without doubt added to the improvement of quality of life for the local population.

Anju fumin and dingju fumin:

The concept of 安居富民 (*anju fumin*) is also often paired with the phrase 定居富民 (*dingju fumin*). Dingju means settled life for nomadic populations. Dingju fumin therefore refers to the prospect of herdsmen living a settled life and becoming prosperous. As was indicated in the above discussion, the goals of "*anju*" and "*dingju*" can be accomplished through the speedy construction of houses and other dwelling facilities. The "*fumin*" aspect, that is, to make people prosperous, however, would likely be more difficult to materialize and accomplish. An analogy could perhaps be made between the concepts of "hardware" versus "software" products and technologies in IT and electronic industries on the one hand and the notions of *anju fumin* and *dingju fumin* on the other hand. The notions of "*anju*" and "*dingju*" could probably be compared to hardware facilities and production that are relatively more tangible and could be accomplished through "structure, order, discipline and control." The "*fumin*" aspect, the goal of making people rich, however, is probably more like the software production that is less tangible and needs "collaboration, ambiguity, and open-ended work situations" (Gregory et al. 2009, 285). The improvement of and investment in software production is usually much more challenging and complicated because they require the transformation of nonphysical characteristics such as human and social capital that are often difficult to materialize. This point has been illustrated in studies on regional differences in China. According to one report, the hardware investment of productive capital accounts for about 19 percent of the development gap between the western and non-western regions in China, but the difference in software human capital investment accounts for as much as 80 percent of the gap (Li, Z. 2011, 84). Another researcher points out China's dilemma, difficulty and limitation in expanding the soft power of spreading its impact in spite of its strong economic influence (Miller 2017, 88–91).

The main strategy that has been employed by assistance teams in Xinjiang assistance program to materialize goals called for by the "*fumin*" (get rich) concept is to try to provide employment opportunities for local residents. Based on Xinjiang yearbooks, *fumin*-related activities in various counties and districts have generated many employment opportunities, providing jobs ranging from several hundreds to tens of thousands in various counties and districts. Projects of wool-carpeting in Hotan with Tianjin's assistance, for example, helped as many as 47,000 women gain employment. In addition, many industrial types of jobs have been generated as well. Zhejiang Province created 10,000 jobs in 2012 and another 5,596 the following year through the assistance program of manufacturing industries (Xinjiang Yearbook 2013, 127, 2014, 116).

What is not clear, however, is the distribution of these jobs between, say, migrants who are usually Han and local ethnic minority residents. Research has shown that Xinjiang's occupational structure and labor market are segregated and polarized according to, among other factors, race, and ethnicity. The Han, particularly Han immigrants, tend to occupy more prestigious jobs while ethnic minorities are clustered around less desirable jobs in terms of income and prestige (Howell 2011).

The Xinjiang yearbooks provide very little information on employment structures in Xinjiang particularly how they are broken down according to racial or socioeconomic characteristics. The following discussion on the labor market situation of Bortala that is assisted by Hubei Province can probably help shed light on some of the issues.[6]

According to the yearbook, a total of 8,540 jobs were created as a result of "*anju fumin*" and "*dingju fumin*" projects in Bortala Mongol Autonomous Prefecture in northern Xinjiang. More than 77 percent (6,638) of these jobs were occupied by migrants and only 22 percent (1,902) were taken by local residents. Furthermore, and more importantly, of the 1,975 jobs that were generated in manufacturing industries brought about by the assistance program in Bortala area, only 223 (11 percent) are filled by people with Xinjiang registration status (Xinjiang Yearbook 2014, 119). In other words, there is an acutely imbalanced distribution of employment opportunities in Bortala. Local residents, compared with migrants, are severely marginalized in competing for jobs generated through the assistance program. As was pointed out earlier, there is little information concerning the distribution of employment and job opportunities in Xinjiang, particularly along the line of the Han versus minority ethnic groups and migrants versus locals. The situation of Bortala can help gauge, albeit indirectly, the serious racial inequality in the labor market in Xinjiang that favors the Han over ethnic minorities.

HEALTH CARE ASSISTANCE

There is inadequate quantitative information on Xinjiang's labor market in official publications in China, as mentioned above. But Xinjiang yearbooks provide very detailed figures on various health and health care-related indicators and measurements since the most recent assistance program. A tremendous amount of resources has been committed to health and health care services and facilities in Xinjiang, according to yearbooks. From 2011 to 2014, as much as 3.97 billion yuan of the assistance fund was devoted to a total of 733 health and health care-related projects. More than 6,000 individuals in health care and other related fields were sent from Xinjiang to the 19 assistance-providing locations to receive training during the four-year period. Furthermore, more than 2,000 medical professionals were sent to Xinjiang where they had provided medical services to as many as 3.37 million patients and conducted around 136,000 surgeries (Xinjiang Yearbook 2015, 132).

Broadly speaking, the following three types of programs have been emphasized in the assistance program to enhance health and health care in Xinjiang: (1) the construction of health care facilities and infrastructure, (2) training provided by the large number of medical professionals from the 19 assistance-providing provinces and municipalities, and (3) the provision of health care and medical procedures and services to local populations.

A large number of health care facilities have been built, expanded, or renovated throughout Xinjiang in recent years, ranging from comprehensive medical centers to clinics, from emergency and disease control centers to pharmacies and patient ward buildings. Health care facilities and medical centers in China are distributed in a rigidly structured fashion with large-scale, comprehensive, and resourceful ones usually located in urban centers and the numerous simple, small, and modestly equipped clinics stationed in urban district neighborhoods and rural townships or villages. It seems nearly every county or city has seen either new hospitals being built or major renovations or expansion being done to existing health care facilities in Xinjiang during the last several years. Beijing, which is assigned to assist one city and three counties in Hotan, for example, built or expanded at least five hospitals, with one being a Uyghur medical specialty hospital in Moyu County. Numerous other health centers specializing ethnic minority medical practices have been established as well, including a Uyghur hospital in the city of Korle in Bayangol Mongol Autonomous Prefecture assisted by Hebei Province and another one in Yecheng County in Kashgar assisted by Shanghai. Pishan County in Hotan set up a Uyghur medical processing center (Xinjiang Yearbook 2013, 128).

In addition to the construction, expansion and renovation of major medical centers in cities, including county seats, an even larger number of medical clinics in rural townships or villages have been built or renovated as well, which is bound to generate positive impact on the enhancement of health in Xinjiang, especially in rural and remote areas. In Pishan County alone, with Anhui Province as the assistance provider, as many as 80 village-level medical clinics have been established or renovated by 2012 (Xinjiang Yearbook 2013, 128). These local clinics are essential in the health maintenance of the vast majority of Xinjiang's population. A clinic in the township of Xiyitidun of Maigaiti County of Kashgar District, which is renovated with the assistance by Shandong Province, for example, "provides basic medical services to 50,000 people to surrounding areas" (Xinjiang Yearbook 2014, 118).

There has been a large volume of two-way flow of medical professional exchanges between Xinjiang and assistance-providing administrative units. At least 6,000 medical professionals from Xinjiang have received professional training in assistance-providing locations and at least 2,281 physicians traveled to Xinjiang to provide their expertise and services. It is claimed that doctors and other medical professionals who have joined the journey to Xinjiang tend to be among the best and brightest for they are referred to as "famous physicians" (*mingyi*), "experts" (*zhuanjia*), or "outstanding doctors" (*youxiu yisheng*). One of the major responsibilities of these medical practitioners is to provide training to local health professionals. As of the end of 2014, at least 133,300 individuals have received such training in Xinjiang (Yearbook 2015, 132).

In addition to offering training, the most important and meaningful contributions of these medical personnel from outside Xinjiang is probably the services and treatment they provide to local residents. A total of 3.37 million people have received medical treatment from the assistance medical teams. These patients were said to have suffered from a wide range of health problems from health issues that are difficult to diagnose or treat to serious and critical health conditions, from existing conditions such as genetic heart abnormalities to communicable diseases such as tuberculosis and hepatitis B. In addition, the medical teams have also provided, free of charge, gynecological, premarital, and prenatal health check-up, eye examinations and other screenings, evaluations and treatment, especially for diseases and symptoms that tend to occur frequently in local areas. For example, hundreds of cataract operations have been performed by various assistance medical teams to local residents free of charge. Many high-risk patients, such as children with severe heart diseases, have been sent to assistance-providing locations to receive operations.

SUMMARY

The recent assistance program in Xinjiang has devoted a tremendous amount of resources into improving the overall well-being of residents in Xinjiang. These improvements are manifested in the large-scale housing construction and renovation, the generous delivery of health care services and facilities as well as enhanced employment opportunities. There is no doubt that these changes help enhance the quality of life of local residents, at least in the short run.

The long-term consequences of these programs, however, are difficult to assess. The readily available aid and assistance that are delivered as material goods and services to Xinjiang can generate unexpected outcomes that may not be completely healthy to the long-term status of the region. One potential problem, for example, is the sentiment and tendency of local residents to be overly dependent on outside help and subsidies. The lack of opportunities and/or motivation to be self-sufficient can make it difficult for local populations and communities to develop sustainable programs and services that are suitable for local conditions and circumstances. The problem may become even more serious when traditional culture and what researchers refer to as "indigenous knowledge" are ignored, dismissed and replaced with dominant "world-ordering knowledge" (Hobart 1993, 1), as will be illustrated in the next chapter by what has been taking place in Kashgar.

NOTES

1. The 592 counties designated as being poverty-stricken constitute roughly a third of the total 1,636 counties in China. Most of them (375 or 63 percent) are located in the western region, with the rest in the central region of China. Slightly more than a third of them (232 or 39 percent) are located in ethnic minority regions or provinces (Central People's Government 2012).

2. Another criterion for administrative units to receive preferential treatment in being admitted into the *fupin* program based on a relatively more lenient standard is if they are located within regions that the Communist Party used as base areas during war periods when the CCP was fighting to gain control of power prior to 1949.

3. Designed mainly to investigate conditions and circumstances of people's daily lives since the reform, the *2010 Xinjiang Survey* collected data from among both urban and rural residents. The longitudinal data demonstrate pattern of changes in the quality of life of both urban and rural populations in Xinjiang.

4. The data in this table may be dated, but they help illustrate the situation of stratification and distribution of poverty in Xinjiang around the time when the Urumqi riot took place and the most recent wave of the assistance program was implemented.

5. The data are assembled by the University of Michigan China Data Center based on 2000 China's census.

6. Bortala is one of the few exceptions that provides information of not only the number of jobs created, but also the breakdown of these jobs between migrants and local residents.

Chapter 8

Kashgar and the Assistance Program

Situated in the northeastern end of the Pamir Plateau, Kashgar is the most far west city of Xinjiang and consequently that of China. It is about 1,588 kilometers from the city of Urumqi and some 4,000 kilometers from Beijing. Until the 21st century, to travel through the Taklamakan Desert in southern Xinjiang, which is one of the largest deserts in the world, one had to take either the northern route or the southern route around the desert. Kashgar is where the north and south routes meet in the western end of the desert, which is the major reason for the city being one of the most important religious, political, commercial, and cultural centers in Central Asia since ancient times. Ever since the large-scale transition of the majority of the Central Asian population from Buddhism to Islam starting from around the 13th century, the city of Kashgar has been an important religious site for Muslim populations in Xinjiang, in China, and in Central Asia. Among the many cultural and religious symbols in the city that are known worldwide is the Id Kah (Heytgah) Mosque, the largest mosque in China and one of the largest in the world, with a prayer hall capable of accommodating 5,000 of the faithful.

HISTORICAL SIGNIFICANCE OF KASHGAR IN UYGHUR CULTURE

Kashgar's prominent position as an economic, cultural, and religious center for Uyghur people was maintained over centuries despite the frequent transition of ruling bodies and power changes in the region. The ancestors of Uyghur people could be traced to Turkic migrants from Mongolia starting from around the 7th century. These migrants and their offspring formed various tribes and forces in Xinjiang in different geographic territories they had settled. The Khocho-Beshbaliq Uyghur Empire that was based immediately north of the Tianshan Mountain range in the current Turpan-Urumqi-Hami area was one of the most powerful Uyghur states. Consisting of numerous Turko-Mongolian nomadic tribes, the Empire not only rapidly rose to power but managed to maintain good relations with China during subsequent Chinese dynasties. One effective strategy of achieving and maintaining this situation was by helping with the Chinese empire's military endeavors. For example, Uyghur assistance played an instrumental role in the success of the Tang government's campaign to suppress the An Lu Shan rebellion (755–763) in China's interior area during the Tang Dynasty (Millward 2007, 36–37).

Coexisting with the Khocho-Beshbaliq was a confederation of tribes that resided in both western and southern Xinjiang, including the Tarim basin where Kashgar is located. Referring to themselves as "khan," which was the "highest Turko-Mongolian ruling title" (Millward and Perdue 2004, 41), these Khanal kings were in control of territories south of Tianshan that extended all the way westward into current Tibet. (Note: Modern scholars refer to "Khanal Kings," or "house of the Khans," as Karakhanids (Millward and Perdue, 2004, 41).) Similar to the experience of Khocho-Beshbaliq Uyghur Empire, Karakhanids' contact and relations with China were among the major factors that shaped the cultural and demographic landscapes of the region of Kashgar. For example, in the year 657, Emperor Gaozong, the third emperor of the Tang Dynasty, appointed a local Turkic Khan to rule the region of Kashgar on the emperor's behalf (Michell et al. 2008).

Viewed from both anthropological and cultural angles, the Uyghur and Karakhanids were separate ethnic, cultural, and geographic forces based on both historical and contemporary evidence (Brothy 2005). Nonetheless, others argue that they should both be considered ancestors of modern "Uyghurs," due to their economic and cultural legacies in significantly shaping modern Uyghur identity and culture (Dillon 2014; Millward and Perdue 2004). The economic prosperity and rich culture of the once-busy city of Khocho, which was the historical center of Khocho-Beshbaliq Uyghur Empire in northern Xinjiang, can be attested even today from its ruins located east of Turpan. As far as the Karakhanids were concerned, they were the ones who initially brought Islam to the area of Central Asia around the 9th century and therefore played an instrumental role in the gradual spread of the religion throughout Central Asia, particularly among the Uyghur. As the economic, political, and cultural center and the royal capital of Karakhanids, Kashgar witnessed Muslim powers thrive such as the Karakhanid kingdom during the 10th and 11th centuries (Dillon 2014, 7). In addition, it also served as the capital of the Karakhitai regime during the Yuan Dynasty (1271–1368) when China was under Mongol rule.

The Silk Road began to lose its appeal starting from the 15th century when maritime travel gradually replaced overland traffic as the dominant route of trade and travel. In spite of this historical transition, however, powerful social changes took place in southern Xinjiang that would generate a long-lasting impact on political, social, and cultural features of not only the region, but its relations with China.

ISLAM AND KASHGAR

With Islam becoming the dominant religion for the Turkic peoples in the area, a unique and significant social institution emerged that was based on the combined forces of Islamic religion and political authorities. Between the 16th and the 18th centuries, the region of Kashgar was ruled by the social structure of Sufi *shaykhs,* an extremely influential religious force that was often combined with local political power.

> This powerful combination evolved into an unusual, if not unique, local form of religio-political authority which elevated Sufi masters (*ishan*) to positions of great power and under which it was difficult to determine whether the populace were subjects of a powerful politician or disciples of a *shaykh* since these roles were combined and blurred. (Dillon 2014, 8)

The legendary leader, Appak Khoja, was probably the most well-known Sufi *shaykh* in the Uyghur cultural history.

Widely considered as a descendant of Prophet Muhammad, Appak Khoja (Afaq Khwaja) ruled Kashgar during the second half of the 17th century until his death in 1695. At the peak of his power, his name was viewed by the populace to mean "the ruler of the world" not only because of the extensive territories that were under his government's control but also because of his popularity as a charismatic religious leader (Jarring 1986). After his death, his descendants continued to control the city for roughly a hundred years, although many of them were either killed or forced into exile by the army of China's Qing government in their aggressive campaigns to control Xinjiang. Having eventually taken over Xinjiang, however, the Qing government realized that it would be nearly impossible for the army of the Qing government to rule southern Xinjiang without relying on, or at least utilizing, the influence of Appak Khoja.

The rich and long-lasting legacies of Appak Khoja and his descendants are most powerfully embodied in the form of a "tomb cult that flourished around the Appak Khoja shrine" (Dillon 2014, 9). His mausoleum at the northern outskirt of Kashgar is considered the "single most important cultural monument in Kashgar; it is a constant reminder of the profound influence of Sufi Islam on the people of southern Xinjiang, the tangible link between the historical Sufi-inspired political and religious authority of the Khojas and the modern Uyghur resistance to Chinese rule" (Dillon 2014, 9).

Indeed, the legacies of the Khojas were so crucially important to the fight for self-rule by the Uyghur people that their presence was essential even when the fights were not directly led by the Khojas. Yakub Beg, a well-known Muslim leader during the 19th century, organized a successful uprising against Qing rule in southern Xinjiang and established an independent Islamic Emirate that was based in Kashgar in the mid-1860s. Despite being an outsider to Xinjiang,[1] Yakub Beg was nonetheless able to maintain his extremely influential, albeit short-lived, Islamic regime (1864–1877) thanks greatly to his skill and efforts to utilize the religious and political influence of Buzurg Khan, who was a descendant of Appak Khoja and the leader of the Sufi *shaykh* in Kashgar at the time. It was also during the reign of Yakub Beg that the shrine of Appak Khoja was reconstructed and expanded. This orchestrated move of showing respect to the shrine of Appak Khoja, however, turned out to be just a demonstration of his astuteness as a political leader: He started distancing himself from the Sufi influence once he declared independence of his emirate (Dillon 2014, 13).

Yakub Beg's regime was not the only independent Islamic establishment in Xinjiang that was based in Kashgar. The East Turkistan Independent Republic (ETIR), even though functioning for only a little more than a year between 1933 and 34, was another one of the independent movements in Xinjiang that were motivated by Uyghur nationalist sentiment. With Kashgar as its capital, the ETIR was borne out of waves of uprisings and rebellions that were taking place throughout Xinjiang at the beginning of the 20th century. These uprisings involved not only the Uyghur, but the Chinese Muslim (Tungan) and other ethnic groups who were resentful of the Nationalist government's policies in Xinjiang such as encouraging Han migration into the region.[2]

INFLUENCE OF FOREIGN POWERS ON KASHGAR

That Kashgar was repeatedly a preferred site to lead to campaigns for an independent Uyghur region was due to the city's rich culture contributed to by many ethnic populations locally and from abroad. To a great extent, these features resulted from interactions with nations and territories across the border, as well as from dealing with foreign agencies and individuals within southern Xinjiang. These international and global experiences have enriched the city on the one hand, but have contributed to political complexity and instability of the region on the other. The UK, Russia/USSR, and Sweden, for example, each left a unique and significant imprint on Kashgar's political, economic, and cultural landscapes.

Great Britain's involvement in Kashgar was predominantly based on the long history of interaction and trade between Kashgar and India through caravan travel across the Karakoram. The British Consulate General in Kashgar, that is, the Chinibagh, or "Chinese garden," was established at the end of the 19th century supposedly to help facilitate trade-related matters.[3] However, it was widely known that responsibilities of the Consul were not limited to dealing with trade issues only. A more important mission was to gather information concerning the overall situation in Central Asia, particularly neighboring Russia/USSR, for the British government. During the slightly more than half a century from its founding until India became independent, the Consulate was an important source of information for the British government's foreign policies and diplomatic relations. In addition to consulate personnel and staff members from Great Britain, there were many Indians residing in Kashgar as UK citizens (Dillon 2014).

It was also at the end of the 19th century (in 1882, according to Everest-Phillips (1991)) that Russia sent its first consul to Kashgar as part of its involvement in the Great Game. According to descriptions of researchers visiting Kashgar during the early part of the 20th century, there did not seem to be much presence of Russian personnel in Kashgar, which was different from the visible and numerous appearances of British at that time (Jarring 1986). But the influence of Russia/USSR on the affairs of Kashgar was arguably more significant compared with that of Great Britain, not least because of its physical proximity to the city. As was discussed in earlier chapters, Russia/USSR had always had clearly defined purposes for involvement in Xinjiang, with gaining access to the vast deposits of natural resources in the region being one of the most significant considerations (Fedyshyn 1957).

In addition to the British and Russians, Swedish missionaries were another group of foreigners that had a significant influence on Kashgar's social and cultural development during the pre-1949 years. The first group of Swedish missionaries arrived in Kashgar in 1892, around the same time when British and Russian Consulates were established there. The reason Swedish missionaries selected the distant area of Kashgar to conduct their projects was because they had attempted to link their missionary routes from the Russian Caucasus in the west to China's east coast, with Kashgar as the connecting point in the middle. Realizing the extreme difficulty of trying to convert believers of the Islamic religion to Christianity among the Muslim populations in southern Xinjiang, the missionaries opted to focus their efforts on humanitarian activities such as providing health care and helping with the general education in local areas. Indeed, according to the memoir of Gunnar Jarring, who was in Kashgar for seven months between 1929 and 1930 as a linguistic scholar from

Sweden studying Uyghur language, Swedish missionaries provided remarkable services to local populations. Poor people benefited particularly since no fees were collected from them for receiving medical treatment in health care facilities run by missionaries (Jarring 1986). The Swedish missionaries also owned the only printing facility outside Urumqi in Xinjiang (Jarring 1986). The ETIR used the press to produce materials and literature for their regime's course (Millward and Tursun 2004), which is just one example how the presence of western agencies shaped the affairs in Kashgar.

KASHGAR DURING EARLY PRC YEARS

When the CCP took over Kashgar as part of the "peaceful liberation" of Xinjiang in 1949, Xinjiang was in the midst of yet more rebellions and upheavals. The Second East Turkistan Republic, or simply East Turkistan Republic (ETR), based in the northern district of Yili in Xinjiang had been established in 1944 under the heavy influence of the Soviet Union. Similar to the Kashgar-based ETIR, the ETR government did not have clearly articulated goals or political orientations. For example, there were debates within the regime concerning the ideal title or preferred model that the government should adopt, be it "Turkish Islamic Republic," the "Independent Republic," or a form of autonomous territory. This was probably one of the reasons for the difficult and complicated processes of negotiations between the ETR regime and the Nationalist government to reach an agreement for the governing of Xinjiang. A coalition was eventually formed in 1946, but it failed to implement the agreement that had been reached. In other words, when the CCP took over China in 1949, it inherited a chaotic and unstable situation in Xinjiang.

A drastic turning point occurred due to one incidence that, from the points of view of the CCP, greatly simplified the circumstances in Xinjiang. In September 1949, a plane that had departed Almaty en route to Beijing crashed, killing all on board, including most of, if not all, key members of the ETR government who had been invited by the Chinese government to attend the National People's Consultative Conference in Beijing. A new delegate leader, Mr. Seypidin, was then sent to Beijing to complete the mission of consulting with the CCP on the political structure and governing of Xinjiang. Seypidin completely accepted the CCP line that the ETR movement was part of the CCP struggle to "liberate" Xinjiang and China, thus legitimizing CCP's policies in Xinjiang not only in previous years, but, more importantly, from that point forward.

With a compliant Uyghur leadership in Xinjiang, the CCP carried out its policies in the region without major obstacles. As part of the overall plan for administrative restructuring and economic development, Kashgar officially received city status in 1952 and, two years later, was designated as the administrative center of southern Xinjiang (Dai 1999, 43–47). These changes were accompanied by intense construction of infrastructure and industrial and commercial facilities. For example, the reconstruction of the 1,350 kilometer highway connecting Kashgar and Turpan was completed within just eight months in the early 1950s (XJKS 2009). The Kashgar Square, one of the city's most noticeable landmarks in recent decades with an area of 41,000 square meters, was built in 1954. Furthermore, fully aware of the importance of the role played by Islamic religion in the everyday life of Kashgar, the CCP also devoted attention to the maintenance and construction of cultural and religious objects. The Id Kah Mosque and the Appak Khoja shrines both received renovation and upgrade during the 1950s.

The speed of construction and development in Kashgar escalated since the reform, particularly after Kashgar was designated by the government as a grade two open city in 1984. Improvement of infrastructure was again at the top of the agenda for development. The 1,500 kilometer highway from Kashgar to Urumqi was rebuilt with asphalt pavement in 1983, making travel between the regional capital and the city of Kashgar much easier. The Kashgar airport was upgraded as well during the 1980s. At least three major boulevards, with a total length of more than 20 kilometers and an area of 480 thousand square meters, as well as three bridges made of concrete and steel, were built or completed in Kashgar in 1999 alone. These transportation facilities paved the way for the rapid industrial and commercial development that the city has experienced in recent decades. The development involved not only domestic businesses and companies but also multinational corporations. One of the first major economic enterprises established in Kashgar during the 21st century, for example, was an 840 million yuan commercial port center invested by a Hong Kong-based company named Xinyifa (新怡发) Co. Ltd. (XJKS 2009). The port city processes and incorporates businesses and services related to port operations such as border customs processing, security, inspection and quarantine services, merchandise exhibition, cargo storage, wholesale and trade market, and other facilities and activities. In addition, under this umbrella company there are subdivisions in such areas as real estate, tourism, and property management throughout the city territory.

As Kashgar was experiencing rapid economic and social changes, its population and administrative territories grew dramatically as well. Historically, Kashgar was composed of two parts that were miles apart. The old city, also known as Shufu or Kanoshahar, was the Uyghur part of the town, and the new city, also known as Shule or Yengishahar, was the Chinese part. The city of Kashgar under PRC initially consisted of four districts of the original Shufu County, and the urban district of Shule County, with a total population of less than 100 thousand people. The population more than doubled from 97 thousand in the early 1950s to around 200 thousand by the mid-1980s and it further increased to 307 thousand by the end of 1999. The current population of Kashgar is about half a million. The urban district of Kashgar expanded from an area of 2.5 square kilometers in 1949 to 96.3 square kilometers in the 1980s (Dillon 2014, 2) and it doubled again to 188.25 square kilometers by the end of the 20th century. Currently Kashgar covers an area of more than 500 square kilometers (XJKS 2009). Much of the territorial expansion was a result of the rearrangement of administrative territories, that is, adjacent areas and administrative units that originally were not part of Kashgar have since been classified as such.

Kashgar and the Assistance Program

When the assistance program to Xinjiang was revised in 2005, it was decided by the central government of China that more emphasis of the program would be devoted to the four prefectures and administrative offices in southern Xinjiang (i.e., Kashgar, Hotan, Aksu and Kizilsu) rather than other areas of the region. While all other administrative units at the prefecture level were assigned only one province as an assistance partner, the four units in southern Xinjiang each were assigned two provinces or a combination of a province and a provincial-level municipality from eastern or central part of China. In addition, various numbers of high-profile businesses and companies in the country were also assigned to the four southern prefectures but not to other units of equal status in the region. Kizilsu, for example, was assigned one company (China Huaneng Group Corporation (中国华能集团公司)), in addition to the provinces of Liaoning and Jiangxi, as assisting partners. Hotan was assigned two corporations (China Electronic Information Industrial Group Company Limited (中国电子信息产业集团有限公司) and China Three Gorges Corporation (中国三峡总公司)), plus the municipality of Beijing and the province of Zhejiang as assistance partners. Aksu's assistance partners were Shanghai municipality and Henan province, plus the following three companies: State Development and Investment Corporation (国家开发投资公司), China Guodian Corporation (中国国电集团公司), and China Shipping Group Corporation (中国海洋集团总公司) (Yang 2010).

Kashgar was provided with more assistance partners than any of the other sister prefectures. In addition to the municipality of Tianjin and the province of Shandong, as many as six corporations and companies were also matched with Kashgar as assistance partners. These companies were China United Network Communication Limited (中国网络通讯集团公司), China Southern Power Grid (中国南方电网公司), China Minerals Corporation （中国五矿集团公司）, Anshan Iron and Steel Group Corporation (鞍山钢铁集团公司), China Huadian Corporation (中国华电集团公司),

and China General Technology (Group) Holding Co. Ltd. (中国通用技术集团公司) (Yang 2010).

Consistent with the pattern of the assistance program in 2005, Kashgar received again more attention than any other prefecture-level administrative units since 2010. First of all, Kashgar had more assistance partners (four provinces or municipalities) than any other similar level units in Xinjiang. Secondly, all the four provinces or municipalities that were assigned to assist Kashgar, that is, Shanghai, Guangdong, Shandong, and Shenzhen, were located in the coastal area and were among the most economically developed cities or provinces in China. There was a clearly laid-out division of labor among the four provinces/municipalities in terms of their responsibilities in providing assistance to Kashgar. Each of them was assigned various numbers of counties or other units as beneficiaries within the district of Kashgar. The city of Kashgar itself was matched with Shenzhen, a municipality that overlooks Hong Kong and is viewed as the most successful case in China in terms of city and economic development since China's reform. The Shenzhen-Kashgar match was the only case of direct relationship of one city as the sole deliverer and another city as the major recipient of assistance in the assistance program in Xinjiang.

The unusually heavy dose of assistance was not the only special treatment that Kashgar has received since 2010. The State Council of China decided in 2010, the same year when the most recent revision of the Xinjiang assistance program was made, that Kashgar would be promoted to become the fifth City of Special Economic Zone (CSEZ) in China.[4] This decision had profound significance particularly given the fact that, at the time of this announcement, all the existing CSEZ's in China, including Shenzhen, Zhuhai, Xiamen and Shantou, were located in the coastal region. In other words, Kashgar was the only CSEZ in a non-coastal region of China at that time.[5]

It was by no means a coincidence that all these events and episodes took place simultaneously. When Kashgars status was elevated to that of CSEZ and when the most recent version of the Xinjiang assistance program was implemented in 2010, China's Hu (Jintao) and Wen (Jiabao) leadership was taking the initiative to enhance bilateral economic relations between China and Central Asian countries (Chou and Ding 2015; Peyrouse 2008). Xinjiang was naturally an important factor in these moves.[6]

KASHGAR AND OBOR

Shortly after the current Xi Jinping-Li Keqiang administration took over power in 2012, it started aggressively expanding China's geopolitical and economic influences in the world. The most widely publicized campaign to accomplish this goal thus far is the One-Belt and One-Road (OBOR) strategy. Standing for "Silk Road Economic Belt" and "the 21st Century Maritime Silk Road" respectively, OBOR are proposed networks of infrastructure and industrial and economic facilities that are strategically constructed along paths connecting China with other parts of the world. Following the route of the ancient Silk Road, the "Belt" extends from China's northwestern region to Central Asia, the Mediterranean, northern Africa, and, eventually, Europe. The Road, on the other hand, reaches Europe via south and southeastern Asia and Indian Ocean.

Needless to say, Xinjiang, especially Kashgar, are expected to be key players in the OBOR initiative, particularly the Belt campaign. This is because, both geographically and culturally, Xinjiang is the region that connects China with Central Asia and Kashgar is the port city in China with closest proximity to most Central Asian countries, including Afghanistan, Pakistan, Tajikistan, Kyrgyzstan, Uzbekistan, and Kazakhstan. The Kashgar CSEZ, consequently, was predestined to spearhead China's global campaigns in recent years and become the hub city in not only southern Xinjiang but the whole Central Asia area. With an area of 50 square kilometers, the Kashgar CSEZ was to be built into a comprehensive urban center with residential neighborhoods, office spaces, recreational facilities, as well as economic and social activities such as technological and commercial development, biotechnology, finance, industrial productions, tourism, cultural exchanges, and production and processing of renewable energy. Very generous incentives were offered to domestic as well as foreign companies to attract businesses to Kashgar CSEZ, particularly those that emphasize new technology, new materials, and new energies. For example, companies investing in Kashgar would be exempt from paying corporate income tax, land rental, surcharges, and many other fees during the initial several years of their investment, and would continue enjoying investment benefit and subsidies afterwards as well. Other privileges include special arrangements to facilitate productions such as natural resource extraction and other heavy industrial endeavors. (Chou and Ding 2015).

As can be expected, the abundant financial and other resources provided through the assistance program are extremely timely and very much welcomed in the development of Kashgar CSEZ. Ten projects were initiated to kick off the construction of the Kashgar CSEZ, with a total budget of 29.5 billion yuan at the beginning of the 2010s. Five of them were directly funded by the assistance partner of Shenzhen and they are all infrastructure or social and educational service facilities including the Shenzhen-Kashgar Boulevard (深喀大道), Kashgar People's Hospital (喀什市人民医院), Shenzhen-Kashgar Educational Park (深喀教育园区), Kashgar Center for

Skill Training and Internship (喀什市技能实训和培训基地), and Kashgar Public Library (喀什市图书馆). (Xinjiang Daily 2011).

The other five projects during the initial stage of the development of Kashgar's CSEZ focus on industrial and commercial facilities and productions and they include the Shenzhen City in Kashgar (喀什深圳城), Kashgar Shenzhen Industrial Park (喀什深圳产业园), the Kashgar Base for Demonstration of Modern Agriculture (喀什现代农业示范基地), the Kashgar Center for Retail and Trade of Agricultural Products (喀什农产品批发交易中心), and Kashgar Cultural Tourism (喀什文化旅游). (Xinjiang Daily 2011). Assistance provided by Shenzhen was instrumental in funding these projects as well. For example, tremendous efforts were made to attract businesses and companies from Shenzhen and other areas to invest in these projects.

Two of the industrial and commercial projects, that is, the Kashgar Shenzhen City and the Kashgar Shenzhen Industrial Park, are designated to be pillars of Kashgar CSEZ (Xinjiang Daily 2011). Referred to as Kashgar's One City and One Park (一城一园), these two projects have received high priority in Kashgar's construction. The spirit and experience of the legendary Shenzhen development have been frequently cited as the reference and model for the construction of Kashgar's One City and One Park. The title of an official newspaper article, for example, reads "(We Should Strive to) Insert Shenzhen DNA into the Assistance Program in Kashgar" (Dai 2014). Two of the most important ingredients of the Shenzhen DNA are said to be "Shenzhen quality" and "Shenzhen speed," which refers to the fast pace and the impressive outcome of Shenzhen's development. The busy and hustling construction site and vibrant activities in Kashgar in recent years have reminded some people of "the scene in Shenzhen during the early 1990s" (Dai 2014).

The comparison between Shenzhen during the 1990s and Kashgar during the 2010s, however, has raised controversies. Some researchers are skeptical about the feasibility of the attempts to copy the development model of Shenzhen and apply it to Kashgar and to make the latter a Shenzhen-equivalent economic superpower and urban center in western China. There are numerous reasons for the skepticism. The most important are the tremendous differences between Shenzhen and Kashgar, as Chou and Ding state: "Kashgar does not have the geographical, social and cultural advantages endowed upon Shenzhen" (Chou and Ding 2015, 128). For example, Shenzhen enjoyed many advantages that Kashgar does not have, such as convenient maritime transportation routes, proximity to some of the most developed economic centers in the world, and abundant foreign direct investment. The most challenging issues that Kashgar faces include the following: (1) the adverse culture of economic development in western China that has been nurtured by the Chinese government, (2) racial tension in Xinjiang, particularly in southern

Xinjiang, and (3) the overall unfavorable socioeconomic conditions of countries and areas across the border from Kashgar.

Realizing the seriousness of racial tension, the assistance program has devoted tremendous resources to try to address these issues. This is probably the reason bilingual education was one of the most promoted aspects in the assistance program. A brand new high school, named Shenzhen-Kashgar Number One High School, was constructed within two years and was open to enrollment in 2015. As of September 2016, there were 3,000 students and more than 200 teachers at the school. As many as eight consecutive groups of teachers and professionals have been dispatched to the city from Shenzhen to offer their assistance with various aspects of the school operation (Hong Kong China News Agency 2016-09-08). Shenzhen also arranged to have 1,089 ethnic minority college students and 1,560 cadres and professionals from Kashgar to Shenzhen and other cities for training and internship in 2012 alone (Xinjiang Yearbook 2013, 131).

Different from most other prefecture-level administrative units in Xinjiang, Kashgar has a solid foundation and resources to support a comprehensive educational system from elementary to secondary and then to tertiary education. Financed with resources provided by Shenzhen, the complete process and setup of educational facilities are referred to as the "Shenzhen Brand Education of 'Dragon' Style from Childhood to College Education" (从幼小到大学"一条龙"的深圳教育援疆品牌) (Xinjiang Yearbook 2014, 120). It means students can experience the complete educational process from kindergarten to college/university education by consistently following the (Shenzhen-style) educational model locally. Needless to say, the most prominent feature of this educational system is the heavy, or total, emphasis on Mandarin language as the teaching medium.

In addition to issues revolving around educational policies in Xinjiang, which was discussed in chapter 6, there is another controversial matter that is related to the "one dragon" Shenzhen-style educational model. Kashgar University, the only higher educational institution in Kashgar as of 2017, is built based on the Kashgar Normal College that was originally established in 1962. In addition to the expansion of the original normal college, much of the traditional old city of Kashgar, inhabited by mostly Uyghur population, has been destroyed and demolished in order to build Kashgar University as well as the many other projects facilitated by the assistance program in recent years. The Chinese government cites safety issues in the old Uyghur town as reasons for the demolition, but observers and many local residents consider this move as yet another indicator of the Chinese government's disregard for Uyghur culture, legacy, history, and identity (Hammer 2010; O'Neill 2014).

SUMMARY

With a history of thousands of years and located in a strategically important position, Kashgar is one of the most influential religious sites for Muslim populations in China and the world. In Xinjiang, it is also the cultural, political, and economic center of the Uyghur people. These are major reasons that it was designated as the power center for the numerous Uyghur independent states prior to the founding of the PRC.

Because of its significance geographically, historically, culturally, and economically, Kashgar has been receiving more attention than other administrative units in the assistance program. Having been matched with some of the most economically prosperous municipalities and provinces in coastal China, Kashgar has been experiencing drastic changes not only economically and in terms of its physical layout, but also culturally and demographically. These changes have generated controversies and debates among observers and they are probably not well received by local populations as well, especially the Uyghur. These issues will be addressed in the conclusion chapter.

NOTES

1. Even though there is much controversy over Yakub Beg's background and upbringing, most researchers are of the consensus that he was born and raised at Tashkent, Uzbekistan, around 1820s (Henze 1989).

2. Also referred to as the Republic of Uyghuristan (Uyghurstan Jumhuriyiti) or, more recently, ETIR, which has been frequently cited as an inspiration for Uyghur people's continuous efforts to gain self-rule. The ETIR, however, had a very short lifespan because of several reasons. Mostly representing wealthy Uyghur businessmen and other individuals of high status, the ETIR did not really win strong support from the vast number of local populations. In addition, the new government had to face an extremely difficult financial situation to maintain not only the government itself but also the military forces that it had assembled. The shortage of funds was so severe that soldiers had to be assigned to individual households for the supply of food and other necessities, which caused even more negative sentiment among the general population. In addition, there were intense in-fights among various Uyghur factions within the regime as well as relentless efforts to eliminate the ETIR by the Xinjiang government representing the Nationalist regime controlling China at the time. All these factors ultimately led to the quick demise of the ETIR (Millward 2007).

3. The British Consulate General in Kashgar was not recognized by the Chinese government until 1908, during which time the government of the UK actually could not even reach a consensus concerning whether or not to continue its involvement in Kashgar and Xinjiang (Everest-Phillips 1991, 23).

4. It would be the sixth if the Special Economic Zone of Hainan Province is included.

5. Horgas in northern Xinjiang was designated as a CSEZ in 2014, making it the sixth CSEZ in the country and the second one in Xinjiang.

6. There is a tendency, however, in Chinese media to credit exclusively the current Xi (Jinping)—Li (Keqiang) administration with the development of economic relations with Central and South Asian countries (e.g., Zhu 2016-09-08). Actually, the earliest efforts by Chinese leaders to engage in interactive relationships between China and Central Asian nations started as early as the beginning of the 1990s following the collapse of the USSR. The Shanghai Cooperation Organization (SCO), or the original Shanghai Five, for example, was established in 1996. Initially founded with the main purpose of strengthening border control and national defense of membership countries, the organization has grown not only in membership, but also in terms of the scope of areas that the organization is engaged in, which includes economic cooperation (Misra 2001).

Conclusion

When the most recent version of the assistance program was implemented in Xinjiang in 2010, China was confidently marching toward a conceived destination that Chinese leaders and intellectuals had been dreaming of throughout the 20th century: a politically powerful and economically strong China. Among the massive numbers of obstacles along the way, the riot in Xinjiang in July 2009 was arguably the most devastating and probably most unexpected. Upon receiving the news about the riot, the then Chinese president Hu Jintao, who was on his way to Europe, decided to cancel his state visit to a number of European countries as well as the participation at the G-8 meeting and flew back to China to address the aftermath of the riot.

This was the backdrop against which the 2010 assistance program in Xinjiang was produced. The biggest carrot that the PRC government has ever offered to Xinjiang, this program has generated controversies from both scholars and ordinary citizens (Sun 2014). During a train ride from Xinjiang to Beijing in the summer of 2015, I had a conversation with several business people who got on the train from a city in Gansu Province that is adjacent to Xinjiang. They all expressed resentment over the amount of resources and attention that Xinjiang has been receiving as part of the assistance program. After all, Xinjiang's economic standing is much stronger compared with Gansu and several other provinces and autonomous regions in western China. At the same time, however, all these Gansu business people expressed their support, at least partially, and understanding of the rationale for the program, as one of them commented, "It is not fair that Xinjiang receives so much support and help. But, on the other hand, we understand that it is for the sake of national security and unity that these policies and programs have to be implemented."

It is not just jealousy that causes the resentment. Those who deliver the aid probably had their gripe as well. As one observer points out, the relatively better off areas in China are actually forced to provide subsidies to Xinjiang (Miller 2017, 71). In order to gain support for the program, the central government portrayed it as part of national developmental strategies that will help with the country's security, stability, and nation-building capacities, as then Vice Premier Li Keqiang stated at the National Work Conference on Assistance to Xinjiang on March 29, 2010:

> The continued enhancement and promotion of the partnership assistance program to Xinjiang are key components of the Central government's policies for Xinjiang. The program is a strategic measure to put into practice principles based on the two general situations and stimulate and coordinate regional development plans.[1] It fully demonstrates advantages of Socialist principles and can help strengthen and develop the unity of various ethnic groups. It is an effective strategy to enhance the region's capabilities of self-growth and stimulate Xinjiang's leaping development. Finally, it plays a crucially important role in promoting tranquility and security and realizing long-lasting peace and stability in Xinjiang. (Xinjiang Yearbook 2011, 38)

The nationalist ideology within which the assistance program is framed seems to be fairly effective in coordinating efforts and soliciting support for this endeavor, as was discussed in previous chapters. With the economic aid as the centerpiece, the assistance program is believed to be an effective measure to cure all social quandaries, including racial tension, as Halper notes, economic growth "is the CCP's ultimate answer for everything" (Halper 2010, 138). Many researchers, however, challenge this notion.

SCHOLARLY DEBATE ON INTERVENTIONAL SCHEMES

The hypothesized causal relationship between the economic development and the reduction of social problems has served as the theoretical foundation for countless programs and schemes by powerful agencies and organizations in many parts of the world. These interventional programs, however, often fail to generate anticipated results. As a matter of fact, many of them are actually detrimental to social, economic, cultural, and environmental features of local areas. Fundamentally flawed ideologies based on the assumption of progressive improvement of human conditions are root causes of this phenomenon, as John Gray so keenly points out:

> The pursuit of a condition of harmony defines utopian thought and discloses its basic unreality. Conflict is a universal feature of human life. It seems to

> be natural for human beings to want incompatible things—excitement and a quiet life, freedom and security, truth and a picture of the world that flatters their sense of self-importance. A conflict-free existence is impossible for humans, and wherever it is attempted the result is intolerable to them. If human dreams were achieved, the result would be worse than any aborted Utopia. Luckily, visions of an ideal world are never realized. (Gray 2007, 17)

Other researchers concur with these perspectives. In his insightful and thought-provoking research, James Scott provides compelling examples to make the point that cultural bias and political motives to promote dominant interest embodied in most of these interventional schemes are fundamental reasons for their failure. The arrogance of planners, unrealistic assessment of local situations, as well as a sense of supremacy are often reflected in faulty strategies and approaches that demonstrate "how little confidence they repose in the skills, intelligence, and experience of ordinary people" in local areas (Scott 1998, 346). Scott also points out that these schemes are usually engineered with a top-down authoritarian approach and very little regard for unique local conditions and cultural characteristics. The lack of trust and confidence for local wisdom and the ignorance of local conditions all help explain the high level of failure of interventional programs.

Hobart and his colleagues present similar arguments. Bureaucratically planned development programs are almost always guided by the assessment and viewpoints of the dominant central power and mainstream ideology while ignoring or dismissing "indigenous knowledges" (Hobart 1993, 1). Consequently, standardization and coercion are measures routinely employed to execute programs that are based on "the developers' knowledge and categories, be it the nation-state, the market or the institutions which are designed to give a semblance of control over these confections" (Hobart 1993, 2). In other words, the ultimate goal of the implementation of most of these programs is to fulfill agendas and interests of dominant political powers.

Unfortunately, however, it is not easy to identify the extent to which interventional programs are dictated by political and ideological motives. What makes things complicated, argues Ferguson, is that interventional schemes are extremely capable of suspending the political and ideological aspects from the execution of their programs, which makes them misleading and deceptive. The routine practice of legal rational bureaucracy and the exercise of the power of state agencies and organizations, for example, are considered legitimate instruments and measures that are often taken for granted in the implementation of developmental strategies. But these power relations and practices usually play the role of strengthening the state power and dominant ideologies. As a result, even when things go very wrong with these programs, as they often do, the planners, dominant institutions, and bureaucratic structures would be able to present the façade that makes them appear as if their only intentions were to benefit local populations and that they had nothing to do with political dimensions, a phenomenon that Ferguson refers to as the "anti-politics machine" (Ferguson 1994).

INTERVENTIONAL SCHEMES IN THE PRC AND XINJIANG

There is no shortage of examples to illustrate the above arguments in the brief history of the PRC. The Great Leap Forward movement that took place during the late 1950s and the early 1960s was one of the first large-scale movements institutionalized by Mao Zedong's regime to stimulate the national economy. But it was so misguided by the centrally controlled government that it was considered to be responsible for the death of millions, or perhaps tens of millions, of people as well as severe environmental degradations in China (Bernstein 2006; Gray 2007, 50). The ten-year Cultural Revolution led by Mao between 1966 and 1976 was intended to improve the Chinese society by enhancing the Communist ideology. It ended up, however, causing such catastrophic destruction to the nation's economy and Chinese people's lives that it has been officially condemned in China as a "ten-year calamity for the Chinese people" (Gao 2008, 13).[2] The infamous one-child policy in China that was first implemented at the end of the 1970s was adopted with the expectation of strengthening China's economy by reducing its population size (Greenhalgh 2005). But this policy was abruptly brought to an end in 2016 because it was considered to be responsible for the outcome that actually hurts the economy: The labor shortage and rapidly growing proportion of the elderly population in China as a result of the decades' long implementation of the one-child policy have been argued to be among major obstacles in China's continued economic growth (Zhang 2017).

The 2010 assistance program is not the only interventional scheme that has been imposed onto Xinjiang. The Great Western Development Strategy that was implemented at the end of the last century by China's Jiang Zemin-Zhu Rongji administration was yet another huge endeavor to fulfill ambitious objectives envisioned by the central government. With the participation of all provinces and autonomous regions in the western region, including Xinjiang, the GWDS was to stimulate the economy of the western region so as to reduce the rapidly increasing socioeconomic gap between the western region and the rest of China as a result of the reform. A huge amount of financial and other resources have been committed to this project. For example, during the first two years (2000–2001) of the campaign, 400 billion yuan, which constituted nearly 5 percent of China's national GDP at the time, was committed as investment budget for this program (Naughton 2004, 267–268).

In spite of the tremendous resources devoted to the GWDS, however, research has shown that the GWDS has failed to achieve its intended goals in nearly every aspect of the program, including increasing the economic vitality, enhancing environmental preservation, and reducing socioeconomic inequality between the western region and the rest of China. Grewal and Ahmed (2011) found that the huge amount of monitory spending on capital construction during the GWDS has not only failed to generate the economic growth in the western region, but it seemed to have been a negative factor in stimulating the economy. Another study that was published in 2010 concluded that the gap between the western and non-western regions had actually widened since the GWDS measured in terms of multiple socioeconomic indicators such as the regional GDP, total fixed asset investment, local governmental revenues, and savings of both urban and rural residents (Zhang and Wang 2010). Research also shows that human capital investment, particularly spending on education, helped with the overall development of western communities, but, unfortunately, investment in human capital improvement was shown to be inadequate in the GWDS campaign (Grewal and Ahmed 2011; Zhang and Wang 2010). In addition, one report shows that while the total fixed asset investment growth in the western region grew by more than four times during the seven years from 542.1 billion yuan in 1999 to 2.19 trillion yuan in 2006, the education funds grew less than three times during the seven years from 6.09 million yuan in 1998 to 17 million yuan in 2005 (Lin and Liu 2011, 9–13). In other words, the discrepancy between funds for social versus economic investment has actually been aggravated by the GWDS.

The problem of imbalanced development patterns that favor the economy while marginalizing human enrichment development is likely more pronounced in Xinjiang compared with the rest of the western region. Thanks to its geopolitical and strategic significance, Xinjiang is one of the areas that have received a disproportionately large amount of resources for capital and infrastructure constructions during the GWDS. One of the largest infrastructure projects associated with the GWDS campaign is the 4,000-kilometer long gas pipeline from Xinjiang to Shanghai. With a capacity of transporting 12 billion cubic meters of gas, the pipeline was budgeted to cost 140 billion yuan when it was built in 2002 (Tian 2004, 12). The amount of gas sent to the eastern part of China made up at least 83 percent of gas produced in Xinjiang's Tarim region, which is the fourth largest oil-producing area in China (Becquelin 2004, 8).

The heavy injection of financial resources, however, was by no means a guarantee of the realization of outcomes envisioned by GWDS planners for Xinjiang, of which regional peace and stability are major components. As a matter of fact, based on the chronological unfolding of the chain of violent events leading up to the 2009 riot, one cannot help but conclude that the drive for the "staged" economic development described by Becquelin (2004) actually resulted in the intensification of racial conflict in Xinjiang (Vicziany 2003). The extremely violent nature of the racially motivated riot in Urumqi in 2009 participated by a large number of mostly Uyghurs was a demonstration of their intense anger and frustration, which is a topic addressed by many scholars (e.g., Clarke 2011; Chen 2012; Hann 2011; Hao and Liu 2012; Millward 2009; Ryono and Galway 2015).

2010 XINJIANG ASSISTANCE PROGRAM AS AN INTERVENTIONAL STRATEGY: AN ASSESSMENT

There is no doubt that Xinjiang has achieved huge economic gains since the 2010 assistance program. Just like what has been happening all over China, Xinjiang has seen dramatic increase in the construction of industrial and transportation infrastructure and living standard of its citizens. The improvement of infrastructure and communication facilities means that the physical distance between Xinjiang and the rest of China, and of the world, for that matter, is not nearly as significant an issue as it used to be. Furthermore, residents in Xinjiang, including many ethnic minorities, have in general benefited from the rapid urbanization, modernization, and industrialization that have been taking place in the region. The increasing number of minority students attending Han schools, known as "*min kao han*," for example, is an illustration that many ethnic minority students take advantage of the reforms in the educational system to advance their chances of improving their socioeconomic status.[3]

All these reforms and policies, however, have failed to change the antagonistic attitude of ethnic minority populations. When Halper reminds his readers of their erroneous tendency to view the challenge posed by China to the Western world in recent years as being military, humanitarian, or economic in nature, his warning is that "The real China challenge is political and cultural" (Halper 2010, 209). The same could be said of problems in Xinjiang as to how they are viewed by the Beijing government versus where the real issue actually is: while Beijing considers economic growth to be the cure-for-all remedy, the actual problem may very well be cultural and social. As another observer comments about China's policies in Xinjiang in a 2017 publication, "So far, economic development and the lure of wealth are failing to satisfy a colonized people craving political, cultural and religious freedom" (Miller 2017, 63).

The negative sentiment and violent behavior of the Uyghur in Xinjiang are reflections of what Clarke terms "permanent provocation," which is defined as the ongoing conflict between China's control and the Uyghur people's desire for self-rule of the region (Clarke 2011). It is likely that the contestation described by Clarke will be further intensified by the assistance program due to the program's lack of sensitivity, to say the least, toward issues that are important to minority populations. The reform of language policies and the audacious disturbance to the natural environment in the region, both resulting from the aggressive implementation of the assistance program, are among the most illustrative examples to demonstrate this point.

CONSEQUENCES OF EDUCATIONAL POLICIES

As was discussed in chapter 7, the pedagogy and curricula of Xinjiang's educational system in recent years, particularly bilingual education, are designed and implemented with the primary purpose of enhancing dominant political ideologies and nation-building. In this process, minority languages are significantly marginalized and suppressed, making it difficult for minority students to excel academically. When Uyghur children are taught increasingly in Chinese only, those who are not fluent in Chinese, which is generally the case in rural areas, particularly rural areas in southern Xinjiang, would find it difficult to comprehend the academic information. Worse yet, when they are routinely exposed to overwhelmingly political jargon and propaganda expressions in the Chinese language at school, which they cannot relate to their daily lives, the effectiveness of their learning is doubly compromised (Tsung 2014).

The problem becomes even more aggravated with foreign language learning. English learning is a must in China for students to be economically and politically competitive after graduation. While the native language is being gradually phased out in Xinjiang's educational system, English has been made a mandatory subject for students as young as third graders starting from 2001 (Tsung 2014, 165). As a result, Xinjiang has to engage in trilingual education. Teachers from local schools in Xinjiang have pointed out that it would be "easier for Uyghurs to learn English than Chinese because both English and Uyghur have alphabetic scripts" (Tsung 2014, 175). This, however, is not an option with the rapid marginalization of native languages in the educational system. Not only do minority students have to learn Chinese, but they have to learn English through Chinese. To many of them, this is equivalent to learning two foreign languages simultaneously.

Due to the strict censorship to do research in Xinjiang, it is difficult to gather information on minority population's reaction to and attitude on the language policy in Xinjiang. But it is hypothesized that there is probably deep resentment and strong negative sentiment against these policies by ethnic minority populations. To a great extent, the resentment of minority populations may be due to the fact that the marginalization of their native languages weakens their ethnic identity. According to primordialist view, ethnic identity is based on indicators such as language, ancestry, religion, loyalty, and emotional attachment. These cultural sentiments are near and dear to communities and populations, especially those that are marginalized by the aggressive trend of western ideologies (Gusfield 1996; Harrell 1997(b)). History has repeatedly shown that even when these ethnic identities and cultural elements were suppressed or eradicated via strong institutional forces, they tend to be so resilient that they would make a comeback whenever there are opportunities even at the cost of bloodshed and violence. The transformation of ethnic identity of the Croats after the dissolution of Yugoslavia (Sekulic 2004) and the Chechen people's resistance against the Russian suppression since the 19th century (Li and Niemann 2016) are just two such examples.[4]

IMPACT ON THE ENVIRONMENT BY THE INTENSIVE INDUSTRIALIZATION

That the 2010 assistance program would generate negative sentiment among ethnic minority populations can also be illustrated in terms of its aggressive campaigns to alter Xinjiang's natural landscape and invasion of the environment through the rapid and widespread construction of industrial parks throughout the region. Industrial parks in Xinjiang are often exact copies of what had been produced in the coastal region. But industrial parks do not seem to be as successful in Xinjiang as they have been in other parts of China. For example, despite heavy subsidies, business tends to be slow in many of the newly constructed industrial parks in Xinjiang (Miller 2017, 69–72). Tourists and observers have noticed that industrial facilities, such as cement factories, are sitting inactive on the Gobi desert because of oversupply of products in not only Xinjiang but also surrounding regions and countries (Cnganta 2017; Wenxuecity 2017). Due to the combined reasons of overproduction, huge financial losses incurred by the plants, and a continuous market downturn for years, many cement and steel plants in Xinjiang have either drastically cut back in production or have to stop production altogether (China Leading Institution of Industry Research 2016).

To assistance-providing partners, the less than satisfactory level of productivity in industrial parks in Xinjiang simply means slow rate of economic return. To local populations, however, the situation is much more complicated. For Muslims in general, money and material possessions are not nearly as highly regarded as cultural elements. To the Uyghur and other Muslims, the Han Chinese tends to have the reputation of being single-mindedly money-oriented, as one of Miller's interviewees comments, "The Chinese have no faith; all they worship is money. . . . But I am Uyghur – Turkic. We are different" (Miller 2017, 70). One of the things that minority populations tend to place great value on is the natural environment in the area they consider their home. Drastic alteration and destruction of natural environment in the region as a result of large-scale industrialization and urbanization have been cited as one of the major reasons for deep resentment by ethnic minority populations not only in Xinjiang (Becquelin 2000, 2004), but in other ethnic areas in China as well (Litzinger 2004).

Furthermore, there is another level of complications resulting from industrial development in Xinjiang. As was discussed earlier, job opportunities have grown following the rapid industrialization. Based on observations of Chinese investment overseas, Chinese companies and businesses are known for their preference to hire Han rather than local peoples for enhancing business efficiencies (Miller 2017, 81). This pattern is known to have taken place in Xinjiang as well where companies often cite minority population's lack of knowledge and skills in performing industrial and technological jobs as the reason for the discriminatory practice (Jacobs 2010; Sun 2014).

DETRIMENTAL CONSEQUENCE OF AID DEPENDENCY

Another potentially detrimental consequence of the large-scale assistance program in Xinjiang is that local areas may become increasingly dependent on aid and subsidies that are readily available (perhaps overly so) through the program. Lack of entrepreneurship and self-motivation in generating business opportunities in local areas and exploring local business culture have been found to be among major reasons for the underdeveloped economic status of western region of China (Oakes 2004; Vermeer 2004). This tendency, researchers argue, is correlated with the high proportion of state-controlled economy and high level of economic subsidies, both of which are prevalent in the western region of China. "The more aid transfusions an ethnic region receives, the worse its anemia gets, as local officials, farmers, and pastoralists develop the habit of expecting, relying on, and asking for outside assistance" (Sun 2014, 235).

Scholars also argue that one of the major problems of the GWDS is that it has failed to stimulate a healthy model for economic development in the western region. By pouring the astronomical amount of financial resources into the region without providing adequate incentives for developing entrepreneurship and private businesses in local areas, the campaign not only failed to stimulate local economy, it actually groomed the mentality and culture of being overly dependent on outside aid and subsidies (Goodman 2004; Holbig 2004; Shih 2004). Given the similarities between the GWDS and Xinjiang assistance program, there is a good chance that the Xinjiang assistance program will generate similar problems.

****

The CCP held its 19th national congress in Beijing in October 2017. During his 3.5 hour speech at the meeting, President Xi vowed to lead the country to realize the goal for China to become a "moderately prosperous society" by 2020. What is the plan afterwards? The following is an excerpt of a direct quote of the official English publication of Xi's speech.

> The CPC has drawn up a two-stage development plan for the period from 2020 to the middle of the 21st century to develop China into a "great modern socialist country." In the first stage from 2020 to 2035, the CPC will build on the foundation created by the moderately prosperous society with a further 15 years of hard work to see that socialist modernization is basically realized.
>
> In the second stage from 2035 to the middle of the 21st century, the CPC will, building on having basically achieved modernization, work hard for a further 15 years and develop China into a great modern socialist country that is prosperous, strong, democratic, culturally advanced, harmonious, and beautiful. (Xinhua 2017 (1))[5]

There are at least two assumptions that underlie the simplistic and seemingly straightforward projection of China's development in the next several decades, as is presented by Xi. One assumption is the taken-for-granted utopian ideology of China's progressive improvement to achieve increasing level of modernization. As I pointed out in chapter 3, this assumption is simply the most recent version of the CCP's ongoing justification for its legitimacy. Since the notion of modernism is so vaguely presented in this context,[6] it is impossible to ascertain the validity of this assumption.

The second assumption underlying Xi's, that is, the CCP's, statement, is that the 1.3 billion people in China marching along the path to the realization of the "great modern socialist China" are identical in their response to the call issued by the Party. If this were indeed the case, there would be no need for interventional campaigns such as the assistance program.

Regardless the outcome of the assumptions and of CCP's plans, periphery regions and ethnic minority populations in China will continue to be at a disadvantaged position. If China is successful in achieving economic gains as it has been for the last several decades, Xinjiang and other periphery areas will have to be playing an even greater role in serving as the power house and supplier of resources for the country's economic advancement. During this process, it is assumed that these areas will never achieve equal status as the economically advanced coastal and inland areas. Interventional campaigns such as the assistance program are designed to facilitate their subordinate status. The assistance to Xinjiang's higher education can help illustrate this point.

Official publications repeatedly state that the goal of the assistance to Xinjiang's higher educational institutions was so they become "advanced in western China, top-ranking in Central Asia and recognizable in the world (西部先进，中亚一流，国际知名)" (Xinjiang Yearbook 2011, 39). These expectations may seem encouraging, but they actually reflect the condescending presumptions about Xinjiang's backwardness and the limited status that Xinjiang's educational institutions could ever be expected to achieve, based on the narrowly defined criteria with the focus on science and technology. Several universities along the coastal region of China are deemed to having joined the rank of "world-class" educational institutions according to these criteria (Yang and Welch 2012), but apparently a bar of much lower standard has been set for universities in Xinjiang. This is, indeed, anticipated as a deficiency by design.

At the same time, it is possible that China will not be as successful as planned in achieving the expected economic gains in the coming years, as Callahan questions: "But what if Sino-speak is wrong? … What if China's inevitable rise stalls? What if Chinese history does not provide a guide to the future?" (Callahan 2012, 52). If it turns out to be the case that China fails to achieve the level of modernization, however it is defined, within the specified time line, there is little doubt that Xinjiang, particularly ethnic minorities in Xinjiang, will suffer from even more disadvantages than what they have been experiencing throughout the PRC era. This is because with the increasing stratification in China, periphery areas are just not as competitive as Han-dominant regions in obtaining socioeconomic resources. Furthermore, ethnic minorities also suffer from a social, cultural, and political disadvantage as their culture, history, and legacy are severely undermined and marginalized as a result of interventional projects authorized from above.

NOTES

1. Please see chapter 3 for discussion on "the two general situations."
2. There is a scholarly debate whether it is rational to totally dismiss the Cultural Revolution as a failure. Xing Li argues, for example, that the Cultural Revolution helped groom many progressive and positive ideas about social justice, political democracy, and human rights that have actually benefited the post Cultural Revolution reform (Li, X. 2001).
3. One important consequence of the educational reform in Xinjiang is the increasing diversity of academic and career options available for minority students. As stated earlier, minority students used to generally attend minority language schools or classes. Since the reform, market-driven forces have dictated that the command of Mandarin language is associated with more opportunities for socioeconomic

improvement compared with minority languages. Minority students in Xinjiang are given the option of choosing between two tracks based on the type of schools they attend. An increasing number of minority students have enrolled in Chinese language schools or classes. While the traditional minority students who attend minority language schools are known as "*min kao min*," this recently emerging and growing body of students are referred to as "*min kao han*."

4. Researchers point out that the primordialist sentiment plays a significant role in Muslim identities. It helps explain the Muslim populations' tendency to emphasize families, kinship, and tradition. Similar to many other religious forces, the Muslim religion also tends to be based on a futuristic progressive orientation. But the aspiration of establishing an Islamic social order is constantly in confrontation with the western ideology of rationality and materialist orientation. Researchers argue that this is one of the reasons for the frustration, anger, and violence demonstrated by the Islamic religion at the global level since the end of the 20th century against the dominant and aggressively spreading western ideology (Lapidus 2001; Li, X. 2002).

5. These two paragraphs are direct quotes from Chinese official Xinhua website in English. The following is my translation of part of Xi's report. The original Chinese version is presented below the translation: Comrades! We have made our strategic plans for the development of socialism with Chinese characteristics during the new era. We will first realize the goal of becoming a comprehensive moderately prosperous society before striving to achieve the level of basic modernization. We will then become a modern and strong socialist country. We must have strong will and perseverance and strive to write the magnificent chapter of the new march for modern socialism (Xinhua 2017 (2) (see original quote below)

同志们！从全面建成小康社会到基本实现现代化，再到全面建成社会主义现代化强国，是新时代中国特色社会主义发展的战略安排。我们要坚忍不拔、锲而不舍，奋力谱写社会主义现代化新征程的壮丽篇章！).

6. The notion of modernization, according to the CCP theory, is based on the unidimensional measure of technological and economic improvement (Cao 2009). This is inconsistent with the conceptualization and operationalization of "modernization" presented in scholarly discussions which include not only economic modernization but also social and political modernization (Fukuyama 2016).

Bibliography

Amineh, Mehdi Parvizi. 2007. "The Challenges of Modernity: The Case of Political Islam." *Perspectives on Global Development and Technology*, PGDT 6 (1–2): 215–228.

Anson, Ofra, and Sun Shifang. 2005. *Healthcare in Rural China: Lessons from HeBei Province*. Burlington, VT: Ashgate Publishing Limited.

Appleyard, Thomas. 2012. "Our Low-Tax Country." *CCPA Monitor* 19, no. 2: 2.

Baiduwenku. 2010–12–24. 全国对口支援新疆工作会议在北京召开 (Beijing held the conference on the assistance program to Xinjiang) https://wenku.baidu.com/view/c9bf89dba58da0116c174994.html.

Baike. 2010. 援疆学科建设计划 (Plans for academic disciplines in Xinjiang assistance program). http://baike.so.com/doc/3842326-4034508.html.

Baike. 2016. 援疆学科建设计划 (Plans for academic disciplines in Xinjiang assistance program). http://baike.baidu.com/view/3623695.html.

Becquelin, Nicolas. 2000. "Xinjiang in the Nineties." *The China Journal* 44: 65–90.

Becquelin, Nicolas. 2004. "Staged Development in Xinjiang." *The China Quarterly* 78: 358–378.

Beijing Review. 8/8/1994. 37, no. 32: 4, 5–6.

Benson, Linda. 2004. "Education and Social Mobility among Minority Populations in Xinjiang." In *Xinjiang – China's Muslim Borderland*, edited by S. Frederick Starr, 190–215. Armonk, NY: M.E. Sharpe.

Bernstein, Thomas. 2006. "Mao Zedong and the Famine of 1959–1960: A Study in Willfulness." *The China Quarterly* 186: 421–445.

Bewicke, Aurora Elizabeth. 2009. "Silencing the Silk Road: China's Language Policy in the Xinjiang Uyghur Autonomous Region." *San Diego International Law Journal* 11, no. 1 (Fall): 135–169.

Blackmore, Charles. 1995. *The Worst Desert on Earth: Crossing the Taklamakan*. London: John Murry.

Bloom, Gerald, and Sheng Lan Tang, eds. 2004. *Health Care Transition in Urban China*. Burlington, VT: Ashgate.

Bovingdon, Gardner. 2002. "The Not-So-Silent Majority: Uyghur Resistance to Han Rule in Xinjiang." *Modern China* 28, no. 1: 39–78.

Bovingdon, Gardner. 2004. "Autonomy in Xinjiang: Han Nationalist Imperatives and Uyghur Discontent." *Policy Studies 11*, East-West Center, Washington DC .

Bradley, Francis. 2015. *Forging Islamic Power and Place: The Legacy of Shaykh Da'ud bin 'Abd Allah al-Fatani in Mecca and Southeast Asia*. University of Hawaii Press.

Brophy, David. 2016. *Uyghur Nation: Reform and Revolution on the Russia-China Frontier*. Harvard University Press.

Caballero, Rafael, Francisca García Lopera, José Enrique Padilla García, and Fátima Pérez. 2012. "Default Prediction for Various National Economies through Synthetic Indicators." *International Workshop on Multiple Criteria Decision Making* 38–58.

Cai, Yong. 2013. "China's New Demographic Reality: Learning from the 2010 Census." *Population and Development Review* 39, no. 3 (September): 371–396.

Callahan, William. 2012. "Chinese Exceptionalism and the Politics of History." *The Journal of Asian Studies* 71, no. 1: 33–55.

Callahan, William. 2015. "History, Tradition and the Chinese Dream: Socialist modernization in the World of Great Harmony." *Journal of Contemporary China* 24, no. 96: 983–1001.

Cao, Fangjun. 2009. "Modernization Theory and China's Road to Modernization." *Chinese Studies in History* 43, no. 1 (Fall): 7–16.

Caprioni, Elena. 2012. "The Harmonious Language of Young Hans in Urumqi, Xinjiang." In *China's Rise to Power, Conceptions of State Governance*, edited by Joseph Tse-Hei Lee, Lida Nedilsky, and Siu-Keung Cheung, 111–137. New York: Palgrave McMillan.

Carter, Ben. 2014. "Is China's Economy Really the Largest in the World?" *BBC News Magazine*, Dec. 16.

Central People's Government of PRC. 2012. 扶贫办发布"国家扶贫开发工作重点县名单" (Thc povcrty allcviation office publicizes "the list of counties to receive poverty alleviation assistance in the nation"). http://www.gov.cn/gzdt/2012-03/19/content_2094524.html.

Chaudhuri, Debasish. 2005. "A Survey of the Economic Situation in Xinjiang and Its Role in the Twenty-first Century." *China Report* 40, no. 1: 1–28.

Chen, Ni. 2012. "Beijing's Political Crisis Communication: An analysis of Chinese Government Communication in the 2009 Xinjiang Riot." *Journal of Contemporary China* 21, no. 75 (May): 461–479.

Chen, Jing (陈静). 2013. 对口援疆的历史演进与绩效评价 (Evaluation of the historical development and effectiveness of Xinjiang assistance program), 中共乌鲁木齐市委党校学报 (*Journal of the Party School of CPC Urumqi Municipal Committee*), no. 4 (December): 21–26.

Cheng, Chao-yo. 2011. "Poverty Alleviation and Development in Xinjiang." *Chinese Law and Government* 44, no. 6: 3–9.

China Daily. May 26, 2003. "China Issues First White Paper on Xinjiang." http://www.chinadaily.com.cn/en/home/2003-05/26/content_166492.html.

China Daily. May 21, 2010. "Xinjiang Takes a Leaf out of Sichuan's Book." http://www.china.org.cn/china/2010–05/21/content_20089335.html.

China Leading Institution of Industry Research. 2016. 2016年新疆钢材市场走势及钢厂复产情况分析 (The analysis of the trend of iron and steel market and reproduction of steel plant in Xinjiang in 2016). http://www.askci.com/news/chanye/2016/03/02/151922in0d.shtml.

China Health Statistics, Department of Health of PRC. 2007. Beijing: China Xiehe Medical University.

China News. 2014. 回顾五次西藏工作会议援藏部署 援藏政策渐进发展 (Reflections on the five work conference on strategies of the assistance to Tibet and gradual development of policies of the assistance to Tibet). http://www.chinanews.com/gn/2014/07-12/6379033_2.shtml.

China Statistics Bureau. 2009. 新中国六十年统计资料汇编 (Statistics collection of sixty years of new China). Beijing: China Statistics Press.

China Statistics Yearbooks of various years.

China Today. March 2010. 56, no. 3: 8–9.

Chinatibetnews. 2015. 中央第六次西藏工作座谈会精神解读 (The analysis of the sixth work conference on Tibet by the central committee of the CCP). http://www.chinatibetnews.com/zhuanti/sixtibet/jd/201509/t20150929_841207.html.

Chinese Academy of Social Sciences. 2011 and 2015. *Almanac of China's Population*. Beijing: Publisher of Academy of Social Sciences in China.

Chou, Bill, and Wuejie Ding. 2015. "A Comparative Analysis of Shenzhen and Kashgar in Development as Special Economic Zones." *East Asia* 32: 117–136.

Clarke, Michael. 2011. *Xinjiang and China's Rise in Central Asia, 1949–2009: A History*. London: Routledge.

Cnganta.com. May 29, 2017. 丝绸之路经济带核心区--新疆水泥市场 (The core of economic belt along the Silk Road – the cement market in Xinjiang). http://news.cnganta.com/show-htm-itemid-280182.html.

CPC News. April 18, 2014. 第八批中央和国家机关央企援疆干部人才进疆工作张春贤出席欢迎大会并讲话 (The eighth group of cadre are entering Xinjiang from state-affiliated departments and companies). http://cpc.people.com.cn/n/2014/0918/c83084-25684998.html.

Cpc.people.com. 2012. 坚定不移沿着中国特色社会主义道路前进 为全面建成小康社会而奋斗 ((Let us) make great efforts to firmly march along the path of socialism with Chinese characteristics and build the whole China into a moderately prosperous society). http://cpc.people.com.cn/18/n/2012/1109/c350821–19529916.html.

Creed, John, and Guoli Liu. 2014. "Coincidental Unwindings: Comparing Growing Economic Disparity and State-Society Relations in the United States and China." In *State-Society Relations and Governance in China*, edited by Sujian Guo, 39–70. New York: Lexington Books.

Crowe, David M. 2013. "The 'Tibet Question': Tibetan, Chinese and Western Perspectives." *Nationalities Papers* 41, no. 6: 1100–1134.

Dai, Junliang (戴均良). 1999. *China's Urban System* (中国市制). China Map Publis her中国地图出版社.

Dai, XiaoXiao (戴晓晓). 2014. 將"深圳基因"植入援疆工作 (Transplant "Shenzhen DNA" into the Xinjiang assistance program. *Nanfang Daily*, 2014–12–19. http://xj.people.com.cn/BIG5/n/2014/1219/c219188–23279811.html.

Dautcher, Jay, "Public Health and Social Pathologies in Xinjiang." In *Xinjiang – China's Muslim Borderland*, edited by Frederick Starr, 276–295. Armonk, NY: M.E. Sharpe.

Davis, Elizabeth Van Wie. 2008. "Uyghur Muslim Ethnic Separatism in Xinjiang, China." *Asian Affairs* 35, no. 1: 15–29.

Desjardins, Richard. 2015(a). "The Precarious Role of Education in Identity and Value Formation Processes: The Shift in State vs. Market Force." *European Journal of Education* 50, no. 2: 134–146.

Desjardins, Richard. 2015(b). "Education and Social Transformation." *European Journal of Education* 50, no. 3: 239–244.

Di Cosmo, Nicola. 1994. "Ancient Inner Asian Nomads: Their Economic Basis and Its Significance in Chinese History." *The Journal of Asian Studies* 53, no. 4 (November): 1092–1126.

Di Cosmo, Nicola. 2009. "Han Frontiers: Toward an Integrated View." *Journal of the American Oriental Society* 129, no. 2 (April–June): 199–214.

Dillon, Michael. 2004. *Xinjiang – China's Muslim Far Northwest.* New York: RoutledgeCurzon.

Dillon, Michael. 2014. *Xinjiang and the Expansion of Chinese Communist Power: Kashgar in the Early Twentieth Century.* London and New York: Routledge, Taylor & Francis Group.

Dreyer, June Turfel. 1976. *China's Forty Millions: Minority Nationalities and National Integration in the People's Republic of China.* Harvard University Press.

Dreyer, June Turfel. 2000. "Ethnicity and Economic Development in Xinjiang." *Inner Asia* 2: 137–154.

Dreyer, June Turfel. 2003. "Economic Development in Tibet under the People's Republic of China." *Journal of Contemporary China* 12, no. 36: 411–430.

Du, Qing, Oyvind Nass, and Per Bergsjo. 2009. "Determinants for High Maternal Mortality in Multiethnic Populations in Western China." *Health Care for Women International* 30: 957–970.

Dwyer, Arienne. 2005. "The Xinjiang Conflict: Uyghur Identity, Language Policy and Political Discourse." *Policy Studies 15*, East-West Center, Washington DC.

Editing Group of Law of Compulsory Education. 2006. *Interpretation of Compulsory Education Law of the People's Republic of China.* Beijing: Law Publishing Company of China.

Everest-Phillips, Max. 1991. "British Consuls in Kashgar." *Asian Affairs* 22, no. 1: 20–34.

Fan, Jin, Xiumei Guo, Dora Marinova, Dingtao Zhao, and Minxian Zhang. 2016. "Assessment of China's Poor County Program." *Journal of Community Practice* 24, no. 3: 264–282.

Fedyshyn, Oleh. 1957. "Soviet Retreat in Sinkiang: Sino-Soviet Rivalry and Cooperation, 1950–1955." *American Slavic and East European Review* 16, no. 2: 127–145.

Feng, Lei et al. 2014. "Distribution and Determinants of Non Communicable Diseases among Elderly Ethnic Group in Xinjiang, China." *PLOS One* 9, no. 8: e105536.

Ferdinand, Peter. 2016. "Westward ho—the China Dream and 'One Belt, One Road': Chinese Foreign Policy under Xi Jinping." *International Affairs* 92, no. 4: 941–957.

Ferguson, James. 1994. *The Anti-Politics Machine, "Development," Depoliticization, and Bureaucratic Power in Lesotho*. Minneapolis, MN: University of Minnesota Press.

Ferry, Laurence, Peter Eckersley, and Wouter van Doorren. 2015. "Local Taxation and Spending as a Share of GDP in Large Western European Countries." *Environment and Planning A* 47: 1779–1780.

Field, A.R. 1961. "Strategic Development in Sinkiang." *Foreign Affairs* (January) 39, no. 2: 312–318.

Fischer, Andrew Martin. 2009. "The Political Economy of Boomerang Aid in China's Tibet." *China Perspectives* 3: 38–53.

Fu, Lecheng. 2014. *History of China*. China CICIC Press. (傅乐成, 中国通史, 中信出版社, 2014).

Fukuyama, Francis. 2016. "Macro Theory and the Study of Political Development." *Scandinavian Political Studies* 39, no. 3: 207–225.

Gao, Mobo. 2008. *The Battle for China's Past: Mao and the Cultural Revolution*. Ann Arbor, MI: Pluto Press.

Gladney, Dru. 2004. "The Chinese Program of Development and Control, 1978–2001." In *Xinjiang – China's Muslim Borderland*, edited by S. Frederick Starr, 101–119. Armonk, NY: M.E. Sharpe.

Goodman, David. 2004. "The Campaign to 'Open Up the West': National, Provincial-level and Local Perspectives." *The China Quarterly* 178: 317–334.

Gray, John. 2007. *Black Mass, Apocalyptic Religion and the Death of Utopia*. London: Penguin Books.

Greenhalgh, Susan. 2005. "Missile Science, Population Science: The Origins of China's One-Child Policy." *The China Quarterly* 182: 253–276.

Gregory, Neil, Stanley Nollen, and Stoyan Tenev, eds. 2009. *New Industries from New Places: The Emergency of the Software and Hardware Industries in China and India*. Stanford: Stanford University Press.

Grewal, Bhajan S., and Abdullahi D. Ahmed. 2011. "Is China's Western Region Development Strategy on Trach? An Assessment." *Journal of Contemporary China* 20, no. 69: 161–181.

Guoqing.china.com.cn. 2011. 教育部关于实施"援疆学科建设计划"的通知 (The announcement concerning the implementation of "strategic plans for assisting academic disciplines in the Xinjiang Assistance Program"). http://www.china.com.cn/guoqing/zwxx/2011-10/12/content_23603501.html.

Guoqing.china.com.cn. 2012. 西部大开发"十二五"规划 (The twelfth five-year plan for the great Western development. http://guoqing.china.com.cn/zwxx/2012–02/21/content_24691623.html.

Gusfield, Joseph. 1996. "Primordialism and Nationality." *Society* 33, no. 2 (January/February): 53–57.

Halper, Stefan. 2012. *The Beijing Consensus, Legitimizing Authoritarianism in Our Time*. New York: Basic Books.

Hammer, Joshua. 2010. "Wrecking History." *Smithsonian* 40, no. 12 (March): 24–33.

Han, Enze, and Christopher Paik. 2017. "Ethnic Integration and Development in China." *World Development* 93: 31–42.

Han, Yuhai. 2006. "Assessing China's Reforms." *Economic and Political Weekly* 41, no. 22: 2206–2212.

Hann, Chris. 2011. "Smith in Beijing, Stalin in Urumchi: Ethnicity, Political Economy, and Violence in Xinjiang, 1759–2009." *Journal of Global and Historical Anthropology* 60: 108–123.

Hannum, Emily, and Yu Xie. 1998. "Ethnic Stratification in Northwest China: Occupational Differences between Han Chinese and National Minorities in Xinjiang, 1982–1990." *Demography* 35, no. 3: 323–333.

Hansen, Valerie. 1998. "Introduction: Turfan as a Silk Road Community." *Asia Major, Third Series* 11, no. 2: 1–11.

Hao, Yufan, and Weihua Liu. 2012. "Xinjiang: Increasing Pain in the Heart of China's Borderland." *Journal of Contemporary China* 21, no. 74 (March): 205–225.

Harrell, Stevan. 1990. "Ethnicity, Local Interests, and the State: Yi Communities in Southwest China." *Comparative Studies in Society and History* 32, no. 3: 515–548.

Harrell, Stevan. 1997(a). "Introduction." In *Cultural Encounters on China's Ethnic Frontiers* Stevan Harrell, edited by Stevan Harrell, 3–36. University of Washington Press.

Harrell, Stevan. 1997(b). "The History of the History of the Yi." In *Cultural Encounters on China's Ethnic Frontiers*, edited by Stevan Harrell, 63–91. University of Washington Press.

He, Baogang. 2014. "The Power of Chinese Linguistic Imperialism and Its Challenge to Multicultural Education." In *Minority Education in China, Balancing Unity and Diversity in an Era of Critical Pluralism*, edited by James Leibold and Chen Yangbin, 45–64. HKU Press.

Heilig, Gerhard. 2006. "Many Chinas? The Economic Diversity of China's Provinces." *Population and Development Review* 32, no. 1: 147–161.

Henze, Paul. 1989. "The Great Game in Kashgaria: Britain and Russian Missions to Yakub Beg." *Central Asian Survey* 8, no. 2: 61–95.

Hierman, Brent. 2007. "The Pacification of Xinjiang: Uyghur Protest and the Chinese State, 1988–2002." *Problems of Post Communism* 54, no. 3: 48–62.

Hobart, Mark. 1993. "Introduction: The Growth of Ignorance?" In *An Anthropological Critique of Development, the Growth of Ignorance*, edited by Mark Hobart, 1–30. New York, NY: Routledge.

Holbig, Heike. 2004. "The Emergence of the Campaign to Open up the West: Ideological Formation, Central Decision-Making and the Role of the Provinces." *The China Quarterly* 178: 335–57.

Hong Kong China News Agency. September 8, 2016. 深圳教育援疆：雪莲花盛开 (Shenzhen's educational assistance to Xinjiang: The blossoming of snow lotus). http://www.hkcna.hk/content/2016/0908/495154.shtml.

Howell, Anthony. 2011. "Labor Market Segmentation in Urumqi, Xinjiang: Exposing Labor Market Segments and Testing the Relationship between Migration and Segmentation." *Growth and Change* 42, no. 2 (June): 200–226.

Hsieh, Jiann. 1986. "China's Nationalities Policy: Its Development and Problems." *Anthropos* 81: 1–20.

Hyer, Eric. 2006. "China's Policy towards Uighur Nationalism." *Journal of Muslim Minority Affairs* 26, no. 1: 75–86.

Ingram, Ruth. August 1, 2001. "Health in Xinjiang." *Central Asia-Caucasus Institute Analyst.* http://www.cacianalyst.org/publications/field-reports/item/7348-field-reports-caci-analyst-2001-8-1-art-7348.html.

Jacobs, Andrew. November 15, 2010. "Economic Aid Fuels Change of Fortunes on Silk Road." *New York Times.*

Jacques, Martin. 2009. *When China Rules the World: The End of the Western World and the Birth of a New Global Order.* New York: Penguin.

Jarring, Gunnar. 1986. *Return to Kashgar, Central Asian Memoirs in the Present.* Durham, NC: Duke University Press.

Joniak-Lüthi, Agnieszka. 2013. "Han Migration to Xinjiang Uyghur Autonomous Region: Between State Schemes and Migrants' Strategies." Zeitschrift für Ethnologie, Bd. Special Issue: *Mobility and Identity in Central Asia* 138, H. 2: 155–174.

Kang, David C. 2007. *China Rising: Peace, Power and Order in East Asia.* New York: Columbia University Press.

Kunlunce.com. January 4, 2017. 金一南：从百年沧桑到大国崛起，从东亚病夫到民族复兴 (From a hundred years of vicissitude to the rising of the great nation, from the sick man in the orient to national rejuvenation). http://www.kunlunce.com/klsp/sp11/2017–01–04/112612.html.

Kunlunwang (昆仑网). September 16, 2011. 援疆工作十四年实践与启示 (The practice and lessons of the Xinjiang assistance program during the last fourteen years). http://www.xjkunlun.cn/zt/zyxjgzzth/2011/2187838.html.

Lam, Tao-chiu, and Hon S. Chan. 1996. "Reforming China's Cadre Management System: Two Views of a Civil Service." *Asian Survey* 36, no. 8: 772–786.

Langegangtie (兰格钢铁网). 2012. 新疆克州赣鑫钢铁烧结项目即将启动 (The sintering process of the Ganxin steel plant in Kizilsu Prefecture of Xinjiang will start up soon). http://gangchang.lgmi.com/html/201206/06/9616.html.

Lapidus, Ira. 2001. "Between Universalism and Particularism: The Historical Bases of Muslim Communal, National, and Global Identities." *Global Networks* 1, no. 1: 37–55.

Lattimore, Owen. 1950. *Pivot of Asia, Sinkiang and the Inner Asian Frontiers of China and Russia.* Boston: Little, Brown and Company.

Leibold, James, and Yangbin Chen, eds. 2013. *Minority Education in China: Balancing Unity and Diversity in an Era of Critical Pluralism.* Hong Kong University Press.

Li, Qinyu李勤余. 2017. 终结高校人才"孔雀东南飞" 仅靠呼吁是不够的 (It is not enough to depend on pleas to end the phenomenon of "the peacock flying to the southeast" at higher educational institutions). http://www.liuxuehr.com/news/jiaodianzixun/2017/0705/29635.html.

Li, Rose Maria. 1989. "Migration to China's Northern Frontier, 1953–82." *Population and Development Review* 15, no. 3: 503–538.

Li, Xing. 2001. "The Cultural Revolution Revisited." *China Review* 1, no. 1: 137–165.

Li, Xing. 2002. "Dichotomies and Paradoxes: The West and Islam." *Global Society* 16, no. 4: 4012–418.

Li, Yuhui. 2010. "From a *Junken* City to a Showcase City – The Formation and Development of the City of Shihezi in Xinjiang Uygur Autonomous Region in China." *The China and Eurasia Forum Quarterly* 8, no. 1: 47–63.

Li, Yuhui, and Linda Dorsten. 2011. "Health of the Elderly Population in Racially Diverse Cities and Counties of Xinjiang, China." *Du Bois Review* 8, no. 1: 53–61.

Li, Yuhui, and Christopher Niemann. 2016. "Social Construction of Ethnic Identity and Conflict: The Cases of the Chechen and the Uighur." *Journal of Muslim Minority Affairs* 36, no. 4: 584–596.

Li, Zhou. 2011. "Western Development and China's Development." *Social Scientific Studies in Reform Era China Ser.: Poverty Reduction and Sustainable Development in Rural China* (1): 53–97.

Lin, Ling, and Shiqing Liu. 2011. "The Progress, Experience, and Prospects of Western Development." *Social Scientific Studies in Reform Era China Ser.: Poverty Reduction and Sustainable Development in Rural China* (1): 1–51.

Litzinger, Ralph. 2004. "The Mobilization of 'Nature': Perspectives from North-West Yunnan." *China Quarterly* 178 (June): 488–504.

Liu, Mingfu. 2010. 中国梦：后美国时代的大国思维战略定位 (The China dream: The strategic positioning of great nations during the post-American age). Beijing: Zhongguo youyi chubanshe.

Ma, Rong. 2015. "Bilingual Education and Language Policy in Tibet." In *Chinese Education and Society* 48: 83–106.

Mackerras, Colin. 2001. "Xinjiang at the Turn of the Century: The Causes of Separatism." *Central Asian Survey* 20, no. 3: 289–303.

McKhann, Charles. 1997. "The Naxi and the Nationalities Question." In *Cultural Encounters on China's Ethnic Frontiers*, edited by Stevan Harrell, 39–62. University of Washington Press.

McMillen, Donald. 1979. *Chinese Communist Power and Policy in Xinjiang, 1949–1977*. Boulder, Colorado: Westview Press.

McMillen, Donald. 1981. "Xinjiang and the Production and Construction Corps: A Han Organisation in a Non-Han Region." *The Australian Journal of Chinese Affairs* 6: 65–96.

McNally, Christopher. 2005. "Sino-Capitalism: China's Reemergency and the International Political Economy." *World Politics* 64, no. 4: 741–776.

McNally, Christopher. 2013. "How Emerging Forms of Capitalism Are Changing the Global Economic Order." *Asian Pacific Issues, Analysis from the East-West Center* 107 (February): 2–9.

Michell, George, Marika Vicziany, and Tsui Yen Hu. 2008. *Kashgar: Oasis City on China's Old Silk Road.* Frances Lincoln Limited Publishers.

Miller, Tom. *China's Asian Dream.* London: Zed Books.

Millward, James A. 2004. "Violent Separatism in Xinjiang: A Critical Assessment." *Policy Studies 6*. East-West Center, Washington DC.

Millward, James A. 2007. *Eurasia Crossroads, a History of Xinjiang*. New York: Columbia University Press.

Millward, James A. 2009. "Introduction: Does the 2009 Urumchi Violence Mark a Turning Point?" *Central Asian Survey* 28, no. 4 (December): 347–360.

Millward, James A., and Peter C. Perdue. 2004. "Political and Cultural History of the Xinjiang Region through the Late Nineteenth Century" In *Xinjiang – China's Muslim Borderland*, edited by S. Frederick Starr, 27–62. Armonk, NY: M.E. Sharpe.

Millward, James, and Nabijan Tursun. 2004. "Political History and Strategies of Control, 1884–1978." In *Xinjiang – China's Muslim Borderland*, edited by S. Frederick Starr, 63–98. Armonk, NY: M.E. Sharpe.

Misra, Amalendu. 2001. "Shanghai 5 and the Emerging Alliance in Central Asia: The Closed Society and Its Enemies." *Central Asian Survey* 20, no. 3: 305–321.

Naughton, Barry. 2004. "The Western Development Program." In *Holding China Together: Diversity and National Integration in the Post-Deng Era*, edited by Barry Naughton and Dali Yang, 253–295. Cambridge University Press.

Naughton, Barry, and Dali Yang. 2004. "Holding China Together: Introduction." In *Holding China Together: Diversity and National Integration in the Post-Deng Era*, edited by Barry Naughton and Dali Yang, 1–25. Cambridge University Press.

Newby, L.J. 1988. "The Pure and True Religion in China, Third World Quarterly." *Islam and Politics* 10, no. 2: 923–947.

NPC. 2001. 中华人民共和国民族区域自治法 (The law of national autonomy of the PRC). http://www.npc.gov.cn/wxzl/gongbao/2001-03/03/content_5004447.html.

Oakes, Tim. 2004. "Building a Southern Dynamo: Guizhou and State Power." *China Quarterly* 178 (June): 467–487.

O'Neill, Mark. 2014. "China Destroys Old City of Kashgar and Builds University." *Ejinsight on the Pulse* (July). http://www.ejinsight.com/20140704-kashgar-university/.

Pan, Yihong. 1992. "Early Chinese Settlement Policies towards the Nomads." *Asia Major* 5, no. 2: 41–77.

Perdue, Peter. 2005. *China Marches West: The Qing Conquest of Central Eurasia.* Cambridge, MA: The Belknap Press of Harvard University Press.

Perlez, Jane. 2015. "Stampede to Join China's Development Bank Stuns Even Its Founder." *New York Times* (April 2).

Peyrouse, Sébastien. 2008. "Chinese Economic Presence in Kazakhstan." *China Perspectives* 3: 34–49.

Postiglione, Gerard. 2014. "Education and Cultural Diversity in Multiethnic China." In *Minority Education in China, Balancing Unity and Diversity in an Era of Critical Pluralism*, edited by James Leibold, and Chen Yangbin, 28–43. HKU Press.

Primiano, C.B. 2013. "China under Stress: The Xinjiang Question." *International Politics* 50, no. 3 (May): 455–473.

Puntscher, Sibylle, Christoph Hauser, Janette Walde, and Gottfried Tappeiner. 2016. "Measuring Social Capital with Aggregated Indicators: A Case of Ecological Fallacy?" *Social Indicators Research* 125, no. 2: 431–449.

Qiao, Tianbi. July 26, 2010. "Assisting Xinjiang is more than Just an Economic Issue." *China Today*. http://www.chinatoday.com.cn/ctchinese/second/2010-07/26/content_286979.html.

Ren, Qiang, and Yuan Xin. 2003. "Impacts of Migration to Xinjiang since the 1950s." In *China's Minorities on the Move – Selected Case* Studies, edited by Robyn Iredale, Naran Bilik, and Fei Guo. New York, NY: M.E. Sharpe.

Rhoads, Robert, Xiaoguang Shi, and Xiaoyang Wang. 2014. "Reform of China's Research Universities: A New Era of Global Ambition." *Education and Society* 32, no. 1: 5–28.

Riphenburg, Carol. 2005. "Ethnicity and Civil Society in Contemporary Afghanistan." *The Middle East Journal* 59, no. 1 (Winter): 31–51.

Roberts, Sean. 2004. "A 'Land of Borderlands': Implications of Xinjiang's Transborder Interactions." In *Xinjiang – China's Muslim Borderland*, edited by S. Frederick Starr, 216–237. Armonk, NY: M.E. Sharpe.

Roberts, Sean. 2009. "Imagining Uyghurstan: Re-evaluating the Birth of the Modern Uyghur Nation." *Central Asian Survey* 28, no. 4: 361–381.

Rudelson, Justin. 1998. *Oasis Identities, Uyghur Nationalism along China's Silk Road.* Columbia University Press.

Rudelson, Justin, and William Jankowiak. 2004. "Acculturation and Resistance: Xinjiang Identities in Flux." In *Xinjiang – China's Muslim Borderland*, edited by S. Frederick Starr, 299–319. Armonk, NY: M.E. Sharpe.

Ryono, Angel, and Matthew Galway. 2015. "Xinjiang under China: Reflections on the Multiple Dimensions of the 2009 Urumqi Uprising." *Asian Ethnicity* 16, no. 2: 235–255.

Sautman, Barry. 2000. "Is Xinjiang an Internal Colony?" *Inner Asia* 2, no. 2: 239–271.

Schluessel, Eric. 2007. "'Bilingual' Education and Discontent in Xinjiang." *Central Asian Survey* 26, no. 2: 251–277.

Schuster, Brenda. 2009. "Gaps in the Silk Road: An Analysis of Population Health Disparities in the Xinjiang Uyghur Autonomous Region of China." *The China Quarterly* 198: 433–441.

Schwarz, Henry. 1963. "Chinese Migration to North-West China and Inner Mongolia, 1949–59." *The China Quarterly* 16: 61–74.

Schweinberger, Albert. 2014. "State Capitalism, Entrepreneurship, and Networks: China's Rise to a Superpower." *Journal of Economic Issues* XLVIII, no. 1: 169–180.

Scott, James. 1998. *Seeing Like a State, How Certain Schemes to Improve the Human Condition Have Failed.* New Haven: Yale University Press.

Scull, Erika. July 7, 2011. "Environmental Health Challenges in Xinjiang. China Environment Forum, Wilson Center." https://www.wilsoncenter.org/publication/environmental-health-challenges-xinjiang.

Sekulic, Dusko. 2004. "Civic and Ethnic Identity: The Case of Croatia." *Ethnic and Racial Studies* 27, no. 3: 455–483.

Sen, Amartya. 1985. *Commodities and Capabilities.* New York, NY: Elsevier Science Pub. Co.

Seymour, James D. 2000. "Xinjiang's Production and Construction Corps, and the Sinification of Eastern Turkestan." *Inner Asia* 2, no. 2: 171–193.

Seymour, James, and Richard Anderson. 1998. *New Ghosts, Old Ghosts: Prisons and Labor Reform Camps in China.* Armonk, NY: M.E. Sharpe.

Sheng, Angela. 1998. "Innovations in Textile Techniques on China's Northwest Frontier, 500–700 AD." *Asia Major*, Third Series 11, no. 2: 117–160.

Shih, Victor. 2004. "Development, the Second Time Around: The Political Logic of Developing Western China." *Journal of East Asian Studies* 4: 427–451.

Simayi, Zuliyati. 2014. "A Study of the Transformation of Xinjiang Higher Education Institutions from the Minority-Han Dual-Track System to the Minority-Han Unification Model." *Chinese Education and Society* 48: 369–379.

SINA. December 23, 2016. 张叶飞拟推荐为镇江市市长 曾援疆任霍城县委书记 (Zhang Yefei, who participated in the Xinjiang assistance program and served as the party secretary of Huocheng County in Xinjiang, is nominated as the Mayor of Zhenjiang City). http://jiangsu.sina.com.cn/news/b/2016-12-23/detail-ifxyxusa4898491.shtml.

Smith, Joanne. 2000. "Four Generations of Uyghurs: The Shift towards Ethno-political Ideologies among Xinjiang's Youth." *Inner Asia* 2, no. 2: 195–224.

Southcn.com. 厉害了我的国！这6张"中国名片"震撼世界！ (My country is powerful! The six "Chinese name cards" shake the world!). http://news.southcn.com/china/content/2017–02/04/content_164647482.html.

Statistical Collection of Sixty Years of New China (新中国六十年统计资料汇编). 2009. Beijing: China Statistics Press.

Subramanian, Arvind. 2011. "The Inevitable Superpower: Why China's Dominance Is a Sure Thing." *Foreign Affairs* 90, no. 5 (September/October): 68–69, 78.

Sun, Yan. 2014. "The Roots of China's Ethnic Conflicts." *Current History* 113, no. 764 (September): 231–237.

Szadziewski, Henryk. 2011. "Commanding the Economy: The Recurring Patterns of Chinese Central Government Development Planning among Uyghurs in Xinjiang." *Inner Asia* 13, no. 1, SPECIAL ISSUE: XINJIANG AND SOUTHWEST CHINA: 97–116.

Teichman, Eric. 1927. *Journey to Turkistan.* London: Hodder and Stoughton Limited.

Tengxunshipin. 2017. 从百年沧桑到大国崛起 (From one hundred years of vicissitudes to the rising of a powerful nation). https://v.qq.com/x/page/g0362dxrj50.html.

Thum, Rian. 2014. *The Sacred Routes of Uyghur History.* Harvard University Press.

Tian, Qunjian. 2004. "China Develops Its West: Motivation, Strategy and Prospect." *Journal of Contemporary China* 13, no. 41: 611–636.

TianshanNet. 2010.克州赣鑫钢铁项目在阿图什奠基 (The foundation for Kezhou Ganxin steel plant has been laid). http://news.ts.cn/content/2010–09/03/content_5207826.html.

Toops, Stanley. 2004. "The Ecology of Xinjiang: A Focus on Water." In *Xinjiang – China's Muslim Borderland*, edited by S. Frederick Starr, 264–275. Armonk, NY: M.E. Sharpe.

Tsung, Linda. 2014. "Trilingual Education and School Practice in Xinjiang." In *Minority Education in China, Balancing Unity and Diversity in an Era of Critical Pluralism*, edited by James Leibold and Chen Yangbin, 161–185. HKU Press.

University of Michigan. 2000. *China County/District Population Census Data Assemblies, 2000.* China Data Center, University of Michigan.

Vakar, Nicholas. 1935. "The Annexation of Chinese Turkestan." *The Slavonic and East European Review* 14, no. 40: 118–123.

Vermeer, Eduard. 2004. "Shaanxi: Building a Future on State Support." *China Quarterly* 178 (June): 400–425.

Vicziany, Marika. 2003. "State Responses to Islamic Terrorism in Western China and their Impact on South Asia." *Contemporary Asia* 12, no. 2: 243–262.

Vogel, Ezra. 2011. *Deng Xiaoping and the Transformation of China*. Cambridge, MA: Harvard University Press.

Wang, Ping. 2016. "Assessment on Language Rights in Education Domain: Shift-Oriented, Maintenance-Oriented or Something Else?" *International Journal of Bilingual Education and Bilingualism* 19, no. 1: 89–107.

Wang, Xiang-Cheng. 2016. "A Critique of China's Gradual Reform." *Modern China Studies* 23, no. 1: 149–168.

Wenxuecity. 2017. 2017回国：第三只眼睛看新疆（2） (Returning to China in 2017: Viewing Xinjiang with the third eye (2)). http://blog.wenxuecity.com/myblog/34338/201705/22622.html.

Wenzhou Dangjian（温州党建）. 2016. 关于援藏、援疆、援青专业技术人员确认专业技术资格有关问题的通知. (Announcement concerning confirmation of professional skills of technical and professional personnel to assist Tibet, Xinjiang and Qinghai). http://www.wzdj.gov.cn/system/2016/05/20/104834381.shtml.

Whiting, Susan. 2004. "The Cadre Evaluation System at the Grass Roots: The Paradox of Party Rule." In *Holding China Together: Diversity and National Integration in the Post-Deng Era*, edited by Barry Naughton and Dali Yang, 101–119. Cambridge University Press.

Whyte, Martin King. 2016. "China's Dormant and Active Social Volcanoes." *The China Journal* 75: 9–37.

Wiemer, Calla. 2004. "The Economy of Xinjiang." In *Xinjiang – China's Muslim Borderland*, edited by S. Frederick Starr, 163–189. Armonk, NY: M.E. Sharpe.

Wilkinson, Richard, and Kate Pickett. 2009. *The Spirit Level: Why More Equal Societies Almost Always Do Better*. London: Allen Lane.

WHO (World Health Organization) and UNDP (United Nations Development Programme). 2001. "Environment and People's Health in China." http://www.wpro.who.int/environmental_health/documents/docs/CHNEnvironmentalHealth.pdf.

Wong, Edward. 2010. "China Unveils Strategy for 'Stability' in Tibet." *New York Times*, January 24, A10.

Wyne, Ali. 2011. "Whither China: Implications of China's Rise for the United States." *Washington Journal of Modern China* 10, no. 1 (Fall): 1–22.

Xiangya. January 27, 2011. 中南大学湘雅三医院。中大人字〔2007〕58号-《关于援疆、援藏人员有关待遇的规定》 (Regulations concerning the treatment of individuals who participate in Tibet and Xinjiang assistance programs, by Xiangya Third Medical School of Zhongnan University, document number 58 in 2007). http://www.xy3yy.com/zcpp/6250.html.

Xie, Yu, and Xiang Zhou. 2014. "Income Inequality in Today's China." *Proceedings of the National Academy of Sciences of the United States of American* 111, no. 19: 6928–6933.

Xinhua. October 12, 2013. Xinhua insight: "pairing assistance" program makes headway in Xinjiang amid challenges. http://www.china-embassy.org/eng/zt/Xinjiang/t1088084.html.

Xinhua. September 24, 2015. "Senior leaders pledge aid to ensure Xinjiang stability." http://www1.china.org.cn/china/2015-09/24/content_36667172.html.

Xinhua. 2017 (1). "Highlights of Xi's report to the 19th CPC National Congress." http://news.xinhuanet.com/english/2017-10/18/c_136688994.html.

Xinhua. 2017 (2). 习近平19大报告全文 (The full text of Xi Jinping's Report at the 19th conference). http://www.coolncute.com/data/page.php?id=1042400.

Xinhuanet. 2017. 第六次全国对口支援新疆工作会议在新疆喀什召开 (The sixth work conference on assistance to Xinjiang opens in Kashgar of Xinjiang) http://news.xinhuanet.com/politics/2017–07/11/c_1121300206.html.

Xinjiang Daily. June 29, 2011. "一城一园"深喀携手打造喀什新特区 (Shenzhen and Kashgar join hands to build the new special economic zone with "one city and one park"). http://xj.people.com.cn/GB/219188/15027765.html.

Xinjiang Statistics Bureau. 2011 and 2015. *Xinjiang Statistical Yearbook*. Various years. Beijing: China Statistics Press.

Xinjiang Statistics Bureau. 2010. *Xinjiang Survey Yearbook*. Beijing: China Statistics Press.

Xinjiang Wenxue Net. December 15, 2010. 援疆干部待遇 (Benefit of Xinjiang assistance personnel). http://www.xjbgwx.com/xbsy/dzcz/677.html.

Xinjiang Yearbook. 2010 – 2015. China Statistics Press.

Xjkunlun. 2013. 国务院关于进一步促进经济社会发展的若干意见 (Opinions of the state council concerning the further development of economic and social conditions). http://www.xjkunlun.cn/dswx/dszl/2013/2778492.html.

XJKS, 新疆喀什. May 31, 2009. 基本完成社会主义改造时期（1952年5月至1956年3月）(The time period to complete the basic socialist transformation (May 1952 to March 1956). http://www.xjks.gov.cn/Item/93.aspx.

XPCC Statistics Bureau. 2015. 北京皮墨工业园区 (Beijing Pi-Mo industrial park). http://www.xjbt.gov.cn/c/2015-01-27/2048902.shtml.

Xu, Zhimin (徐志民). May 15, 2015. 援藏：党的民族政策实践的成功典范 (Assistance to Tibet: A successful model of the implementation of the party's ethnic policies). *Social Science in China Press* 738. http://sscp.cssn.cn/xkpd/tbch/tebiecehuaneirong/201505/t20150515_1826838.html.

Yang, Fuqiang. 杨富强. 2008. 对新时期援疆政策的社会学思考 (Sociological analysis of policies of Xinjiang assistance program during the new era). http://mall.cnki.net/magazine/Article/XXBL200808080.html.

Yang, Fuqiang. 杨富强. 2010. 对口援疆政策回顾及思考，以1997–2000年间政策实践为例 (Partnership assistance program in Xinjiang: Policy review and reflection, 1997–2000). 西北民族大学学报 (*Journal of Northwestern University*) 5: 1–5.

Yang, Rui, and Anthony Welch. 2010. "A World-Class University in China: The Case of Tsinghua." *Higher Education* 63: 465–666.

Yaxin. 2010. 对口支援新疆工作基本情况 (Basic conditions of partnership assistance to Xinjiang). http://zt.iyaxin.com/content/2010–04/20/content_1715023.html.

Yaynen, Jennifer. 2006. "Interpreters, Arbiters or Outsiders: The Role of the *Min kao Han* in Xinjiang Society." *Journal of Muslim Minority Affairs* 26, no. 1: 45–62.

Yee, Herbert. 2005. "Ethnic Consciousness and Identity, a Research Report on Uyghur-Han Relations in Xinjiang." *Asian Ethnicity* 6, no. 1: 35–50.

Yuan, Fang et al. 2015. "Analysis of Awareness of Health Knowledge among Rural Residents in Western China." *BMC Public Health*: 15: 55. https://doi.org/10.1186/s12889–015–1393–2.

Zeng, Yi, Dudley Poston, Denise Ashbaugh Vlosky, and Danan Gu, eds. 2008. *Healthy Longevity in China: Demographic, Socioeconomic, and Psychological Dimensions.* New York: Springer Publisher.

Zhang, Junsen. 2017. "The Evolution of China's One-Child Policy and Its Effects on Family Outcomes." *The Journal of Economic Perspectives* 31, no. 1: 141–159.

Zhang, Lijun, and Wang Fei. 2010. "Current State of Economic Returns from Education in China's Ethnic Regions and Explorations into Ways of Improvement." *Chinese Education and Society* 43, no. 5: 10–30.

Zhao, Minggang. 2011. 中国特色对口支援模式研究 (The study of partnership Assistance program with Chinese characteristics). http://doc.qkzz.net/article/4b82b069-b83b-42f0–81f0–91f21e0664ed.html.

Zhao, Suisheng. 1993. "Deng Xiaoping's Southern Tour: Elite Politics in Post-Tiananmen China." *Asian Survey* 33, no. 8: 739–756.

Zhu, Guoren. 朱国仁. 2016-09-08. "一带一路"的创新意义。人民日报海外版. (The innovative significance of "one road one belt," overseas edition of *People's Daily*, September 8, 2016). http://media.china.com.cn/cmjujiao/2016–09–08/853032.html.

Zinan. December 22, 2010. 市卫生局召开第七批卫生援疆干部工作会 (Municipality Health Department Holds a Conference to Commemorate the 7th Group of Cadre to Assist Xinjiang). http://www.54md.com/news/n17/357374.html.

Index

About the Author

Yuhui Li is a professor of Sociology at Rowan University in the United States. She obtained her doctoral degree in Sociology from Ohio State University. Her teaching and research areas include sociological research methods, ethnic relations, community and regional development in China, and social demography.